LAW ENFORCEMENT MANAGEMENT

What Works and What Doesn't

MICHAEL CARPENTER
ROGER FULTON

43-08 162nd Street
Flushing, NY 11358
www.LooseleafLaw.com
800-647-5547

Library of Congress Cataloging-In-Publication Data

Carpenter, Michael J.
Law enforcement management : what works and what doesn't! / Michael Carpenter and Roger Fulton.
p. cm.
Includes index.
ISBN 978-1-932777-90-1
1. Police--Supervision of. 2. Police administration. 3. Law enforcement.
I. Fulton, Roger. II. Title.
HV7936.S8C37 2010
363.2'2--dc22

2009048276

2nd Printing, 2010
3rd Printing, 2011
4th Printing, 2013
5th Printing, 2015
6th Printing, 2017
7th Printing, 2018

Cover design by *Sans Serif, Inc.* Saline, Michigan

About the Authors

Michael Carpenter

Michael Carpenter has more than thirty years experience in various law enforcement related positions, having worked with a municipal police department, a state police agency, as a statewide police specialist for the State of New York, and is currently a full-time professor of criminal justice at Adirondack Community College in upstate New York.

He started his career with a city police department, and then worked with a state police agency for more than ten years as a trooper, as an investigator, and as a sergeant. Later hired by the State of New York as a "police training specialist," he assisted in developing and implementing the country's first state-sponsored law enforcement accreditation program. He assisted more than 65 agencies achieve accreditation or re-accreditation status. For several years, he also prepared detailed management studies of police departments for the State of New York and offered specific recommendations to resolve various administrative or operational issues that these agencies faced.

In addition to practical experience, he holds a Master's Degree in Criminal Justice and a Master's Degree in Teaching and has more than ten years experience in supervisory and administrative positions. He has been a certified police instructor for more than twenty years and was an adjunct college instructor for more than ten years.

He has written several books, edited several books, has had more than 100 articles or columns published in national criminal justice publications, has taught in college classrooms, made presentations at national conferences, and worked as a private consultant. He is also the founder of a successful police consulting service called Police Management Services. He can be contacted through his webpage at *www.policemanagement.com*.

Roger Fulton
Captain, New York State Police (Ret.)

Roger Fulton has dedicated himself to police professionalism for more than thirty years. He quickly rose through the ranks of the New York State Police to the rank of captain. During his career, he held numerous command and administrative positions.

Roger holds a Ph.D. in Criminal Justice Management, a Master's Degree in Criminal Justice, and is a graduate of the FBI's National Academy (139th Session). In addition to his education and training, he has years of practical supervisory and management experience in both the public and private sectors. In recent years, he has traveled extensively from Florida to Alaska and from California to New Jersey as a consultant, advisor, and trainer for police departments and academies throughout the nation.

He is the author of three successful books, *Common Sense Management, A Practical Career Guide for Criminal Justice Professionals*, and now, coauthor of *Law Enforcement Management—What Works and What Doesn't.* He was also a columnist for *Law Enforcement Technology* magazine for twelve years writing on police supervision, management, and leadership issues.

Contact him through his webpage at: *www.RogerFulton.com*.

Table of Contents

memorize list
and order they
ar in.

Chapter 1
INTRODUCTION

This book has been designed as a guide for law enforcement personnel who are upwardly mobile and want to become good supervisors, managers, and leaders in their chosen profession. That career path can be challenging, but we hope that this book makes it a little easier for you.

Chapter 2 starts with *"Getting Ready,"* which helps you prepare for a promotion.

As Abraham Lincoln once said:

I will prepare and my time will come.

Chapter 3 assumes that you did prepare and you got promoted to a supervisory position in your department. Good job! But now what? We explore the challenges that await you.

Chapters 4 through 7 help you cope with the daily demands of being a law enforcement supervisor or manager.

Chapter 8 covers some of the problems and pitfalls you may encounter in dealing with personnel problems.

Chapter 9, *"Leading the Way,"* provides advice for true success in your career. Read it and heed it! It will be of great value to you throughout your entire career.

Chapter 10, *"Job Security,"* should help you avoid some of the career-ending pitfalls inherent in your job.

We realize that at some point you will retire (hopefully on your own terms!). We want you to appreciate the fact that there is life *after* you retire, and we want you to be aware of, and plan ahead for, that major step in your life. Thus, **Chapter 11**, *"Your Future,"* provides some tips for that stage of your career.

Although there is much more you can do and learn for a successful career in law enforcement, we have presented what we can to help you build a successful career. The rest is up to you to follow our advice and add your own experiences to it.

Leadership and learning are indispensable to each other.
— John F. Kennedy

Chapter 2
GETTING READY

Before anything else, preparation is the key to success.
— Alexander Graham Bell

Section 1 — Understanding Your Organization

Can you picture a patrol sergeant being pulled from his shift to go negotiate the department's budget with the city council? How about the police commissioner being assigned to handle a robbery in progress at a local liquor store?

Both of these scenarios are highly unlikely in most departments. That's because we all have fairly well-defined duties and responsibilities that are set out by our titles and positions within the department.

However, in order to be truly successful at any rank, you must know not only your own job, but also how the other components contribute to the overall success of the organization. This general understanding allows you to concentrate on your own duties, while referring other duties to those who specialize in them, and who presumably can perform them better.

In general terms, upper-level management (commissioners, chiefs, superintendents), are responsible for ensuring that the department fulfills its overall mission of maintaining order and controlling criminal activity. To do this, their duties include obtaining the resources (money, staff, and equipment) that allow everyone else in the department to perform their jobs effectively.

Mid-level managers, generally lieutenants and captains, are most often responsible for the planning and coordination activities of the department. They set medium-term goals and objectives and ensure that those goals and objectives are reached by their respective divisions.

Line-level supervisors (corporals and sergeants) are responsible for the day-to-day implementation of policies and procedures by patrol officers and detectives. The activities they oversee (patrol, call response, investigation, apprehension of offenders, etc.) are the individual activities that, when taken collectively, add up to the successful performance of the department.

In addition to these main categories, there are other people who contribute to the success of the organization, including staff and support personnel. These groups include specialists, as well as other employees who do their part to make the department run smoothly. The number of these staff and support personnel usually depends on the size of the department, as well as any special duties assigned to the department. Most departments couldn't run effectively without these personnel.

When you examine the activities of each individual component in the department, you quickly realize that all of the segments are interdependent. Line personnel must have the resources to succeed, as much as senior management must rely on all of the various components to perform their jobs adequately. At the same time, staff and support positions tend to make everyone's life a little easier.

Knowing what everyone in the organization does, and how they interact, can help you to understand the organization as a whole. You will also be able to clearly see what is expected from you, as well as what you should expect from others.

Understanding your organization won't solve all of your day-to-day problems, but it certainly is a good start.

Section 2 — Do You Know Your Policies?

One of your department's patrols is attempting to stop a vehicle for a traffic violation, but it refuses to pull over. They are going only 30 miles per hour, but when a second patrol car gets in front of the violator, the violator rams the back of the patrol car and turns down a side street to escape.

What departmental policies now cover the supervisor's actions, and the actions of the patrol officers? Everyone involved had better already know, because it's too late to look them up now!

Too many officers and supervisors are unfamiliar with their own department's policies, many of which directly involve the use of force.

Here's a quick list of questions a good supervisor should be able to answer regarding the policies and procedures of their department.

Pursuit

Can patrols pursue for a traffic violation? A misdemeanor? A felony? Or do you have a "no pursuit" policy? If so, what else can they do? Are there speed restrictions on pursuits? What are they?

What does a supervisor do during a pursuit? Is the number of cars limited by policy? What about other departments' cars involved in the pursuit? Who is in charge of them?

Who is ultimately responsible for the pursuit and any consequences of it?

Use of Deadly Force

What if the occupants of the vehicle shoot at the police patrols? Are there restrictions on shooting at, or from, a moving vehicle? Can the patrols use warning shots?

Is departmental policy different from the statutory justification law? How? Does the level of crime involved make a difference in what can be done? What about third parties whose lives are in danger?

Can a baton blow constitute deadly physical force? What about a blow from a flashlight? What are a supervisor's duties if deadly force is used by an officer?

Forcible Stopping of Vehicles

What is legal intervention? Is there authority for it? Where? Can your patrols ram a car? Under what circumstances? Does that constitute the use of deadly force?

Can you set up a roadblock? Moving roadblocks? Fixed roadblocks? What about "Spike Strips?" Are roadblocks deadly force?

Can you shoot out tires? Gas tanks? Will either do any good? Who is ultimately responsible for the forcible stopping of a vehicle and any consequences?

If you can answer every one of these questions without hesitation, then feel secure that you can handle the opening scenario as an officer or as a supervisor with confidence. Does every officer and every supervisor in your department know the answers to every one of these questions? Otherwise, you may want to call off the pursuit until everyone in the department can look up some of the policies and procedures they aren't quite sure they have read recently.

Violating departmental policies is a surefire way to jeopardize officer and civilian lives, as well as possibly ending an officer's or supervisor's career!

Section 3 — Getting Along With the Boss

It's a simple fact of life. Everyone has a boss.

The patrol officer has a sergeant; the sergeant has a lieutenant; the captain has the chief, and the chief has the mayor or city manager.

Regardless of where you fall in the hierarchy of your organization, it is to your advantage to get along with your boss. Failure to maintain an adequate working relationship can result in a difficult job situation, at its best. At its worst, it can end up with you standing in the unemployment line.

To help you avoid the latter, here are a few hints that can help you to maintain a good working relationship with your boss, regardless of who it is.

Don't Be Afraid of the Boss

The boss needs you as much as you need the boss. Remember that the boss's job is to get things done through people. You are one of those people. Just as he or she can be a key to your success, your excellent performance is necessary for the boss's success.

All Bosses Have Quirks

Just as you have your idiosyncrasies, so do they. Learn their quirks and learn to work with them. As a rule, you are the one who must adapt because the bosses probably aren't going to change to suit your idiosyncrasies. After all, they are the bosses!

Bosses Don't Like Surprises

Keep them informed about potential problem areas. Let them know that you are aware of the potential problem and that you are taking steps to control it. Don't let bosses find out there is a serious impending problem in your area from someone else!

Don't Try to Hide a Problem

If the problem finally arrives, then handle it. Let the boss know as soon as possible that you have a serious problem. Tell the boss what solutions you propose, and ask for any additional recommendations they might have. You'll be surprised at how supportive the boss will be.

Use the Boss's Time Effectively

Chances are there are several people like you reporting to the same boss. Therefore, your time with the boss is limited. Use just enough of it to get the information and guidance you need. Before going in, write down what you need to discuss and what you need from the boss.

Be ready to answer simple questions. When you have what you need, it's time to leave—unless the boss wants to discuss something more with you.

Follow Up Your Meeting in Writing

After a meeting with your boss, it may be appropriate to follow up with a short memo or e-mail outlining what was discussed and what actions you both agreed to take. This gives you both a last chance option in case there were any misunderstood communications during your meeting.

Never Embarrass the Boss—*NEVER!*

Many embarrassing situations are caused because the boss doesn't know about something, and therefore isn't prepared to handle it in front of peers, superiors, or the press. Your foresight in warning your boss of potentially embarrassing situations can go a long way to building a strong and trusting relationship, especially if you aren't the cause of the potential embarrassment.

Maintaining a good overall relationship with your boss can make both of your jobs much easier and more enjoyable. All it takes is a little understanding, a little tolerance, and some good, old-fashioned common sense on your part.

Section 4 — Learning Supervisory Skills

Police commanders want all of their supervisors in the department to be knowledgeable and capable professionals. They want them to make good decisions and to exhibit excellent supervisory skills. That doesn't "just happen."

Most skills and abilities that we generally consider necessary to becoming a good police supervisor can be learned. Most newly promoted sergeants and lieutenants *will* learn these skills over time. But a police commander needs those good supervisors now, not ten years from now.

Because most of the necessary skills are learned, an understanding of how new supervisors learn those skills can give you some ideas on how to accelerate the learning process. To that end, here are several of the methods supervisors use to learn their supervisory skills.

Observations of Their Supervisors

In most departments everyone starts out as a line police officer and often spends years in that position before they are promoted. During that time, they are constantly watching and evaluating the actions and performance of their supervisors in routine matters, as well as during critical police incidents. From those observations, they draw their own conclusions, and their collective experiences over the years help shape their supervisory personality for the future.

But for this type of learning to work best, those patrol officers need to watch knowledgeable, capable, and professional supervisors who have learned excellent supervisory skills. That is not always the case. As one young sergeant told his captain, "My sergeant always screamed at me at lineup if I did a bad report or something. So when I made sergeant, I did the same thing to my officers. It was a long time before I learned the proper way of praising in public and chastising in private. Now I know."

Policy and Procedure Manuals

Most progressive police departments have developed extensive policy and procedure manuals to guide all members of the department in their everyday activities. And many departments require promotional candidates to display adequate knowledge of the content of those manuals, generally through some type of a competitive written or oral exam. This process makes good sense for some of the technical aspects of their work, but it does little to help them learn supervisory skills.

Although some of the policies and procedures have some relationship to personnel actions and decisions, they cannot help the candidate to develop the person-to-person supervisory skills so necessary to becoming a successful supervisor. Besides, they were studying those manuals primarily to pass the test, not studying how to be an effective supervisor. Therefore they may not have focused on the value of the long-term effects of what they were reading.

Formal Training Courses

Few states require any specific training courses for new police supervisors. Even those that do vary widely in their specific hourly or course content standards. Therefore, it is left to the local department or regional academy to provide such training. Many don't.

To put a police officer on the street without basic academy training is unthinkable in today's modern policing environment. Yet new police supervisors are often thrust into their new positions with little or no training courses to help them learn supervisory skills. Commanders would do well to ensure that those who will soon be promoted are given adequate basic supervisory skills training prior to assuming their new positions. Such training may help prevent problems for the new supervisor, as well as in helping prevent long-term problems for you.

On-the-Job Training

After police recruits complete the basic academy, they are sent on to a field training program to work with a senior officer for a period of time. Many progressive police departments conduct a similar field training officer (FTO) program for new supervisors.

This type of program allows them to work with an excellent, experienced supervisor who can help them translate their past experience, and their new supervisory training, into sound supervisory practices. The people skills they learn from an experienced and professional supervisor during this segment of their training will serve them well throughout their careers.

Trial and Error

This method of learning is the new police supervisor's least favorite way to learn. The "trial" part causes them stress and the "error" part causes them even more stress. When things go wrong, they can go very wrong, very quickly. Yet it can take years to climb the learning curve to successful supervision using this learning method. Forcing them to use this method is setting them up for failure from the beginning in their new position.

Police commanders should do everything they can to help their new supervisors learn the skills required of a police supervisor before ever promoting them. Doing so will prevent both short- and long-term problems for the new supervisor, for their commanders, and for the department.

Section 5 — Do Police Supervisors Need College Degrees?

When more than 500 active police sergeants, lieutenants, and captains were asked if they should be required to have college degrees, the majority said, "yes." When they were then asked to briefly explain their answers in writing, the results got much more interesting.

The police supervisors surveyed were selected at random from small, medium, and large agencies across the country. The survey was conducted anonymously so respondents could provide honest, candid, and straightforward answers. As a result, their responses were just that, both pro and con.

A sergeant from a small department in Virginia responded that a college degree should not be required of police supervisors. He then wrote, "A good supervisor with a thorough knowledge of his job and good people skills does not need a degree to do the job, but it also couldn't hurt to further his or her education."

From a medium-sized sheriff's department in Florida, a sergeant with 18 years of experience in the sergeant's rank indicated, "Yes," police supervisors should be required to have college degrees. He wrote, "Supervisors must be able to communicate and to review others' communications. College prepares the individual for those skills."

These two differing responses were typical for those who hold the rank of sergeant. Survey results showed that 52% of the sergeants said "yes" to a college degree requirement, while 47% said "no," and 1% did not answer. Lieutenants voted their preferences in almost the exact same percentages.

However, those holding the rank of captain and above placed more emphasis on requiring a college degree for supervisors, with nearly two thirds of them saying "yes" to a degree requirement.

From a large county agency in Maryland, a captain wrote, "The communications skills, both verbal and written, are needed to be effective and require advanced education." He holds a Master's Degree.

Yet another captain from a small department in New York said "no" to the degree requirement and stated, "I feel high school and experiences on the job is good enough." He has no degree.

A police chief who worked his way up through the ranks, working at least five years each as a sergeant, a lieutenant, a captain, and a chief, voted "yes" for a degree requirement. "Today's demands on police supervisors make it essential," he stated. He has a Bachelor's Degree.

Although the number of supervisors in favor of a degree requirement represented the majority view, even many of those answering "no" to the degree requirement thought college was a good idea.

Here are some of the dissenting opinions:

A six-year sergeant from Wisconsin stated, *"No requirement—but it should be urged and the promotional process should give some weight to it."*

A sergeant from Delaware stated, *"Am in between the 'yes' and 'no.' I firmly believe in continuing one's education. However, I have seen supervisors who have had degrees who had no business being supervisors. I have also seen supervisors who did not have a degree and I would be very content to work under them."*

A sergeant from Illinois, who holds a Bachelor's degree, wrote, *"I don't believe a college degree is required if the individual has demonstrated the necessary skills to be a good supervisor."*

Many of those in favor of a degree requirement were very articulate in citing their reasons. Here are some examples:

A 12-year lieutenant from Massachusetts wrote, *"The world is changing. The job is changing. The public expects educated police supervisors. The writing and other skills learned are as valuable as the degree."*

A 23-year lieutenant from Tennessee answered "yes," and explained why. *"In an information-based age such as the one in which we live, and which will only become more demanding in the near future, supervisors must be able to deal in a more complex and diverse social environment."*

An eight-year sergeant from a medium-sized agency in Texas stated, *"The process of obtaining a college degree instills particular qualities which are valuable to a supervisor. These qualities include organizational skills, planning and the ability to follow through with a long-term project. You are also given opportunities to interact with a wide variety of people."*

The greatest single indicator as to whether or not a respondent would answer "yes" or "no" to the degree requirement was their own degree of education. Among supervisors who had "high school only," only 24% felt a college degree was necessary. But, among those who hold a "Master's degree or above," 78% felt there should be a degree requirement for police supervisors.

However, a 29-year veteran from Iowa, with 20 years as a sergeant, summed up the views of the majority of respondents, whether they voted "yes" or "no" for a degree requirement. He cited four reasons to have college-educated police supervisors.

(1) "The public expects it as the general population is becoming more educated.

(2) More line officers have degrees. They have little respect for supervisors who don't.

(3) The term professionalism requires some standard to begin with. Education is usually one of the building points.

(4) Better employees."

The sergeant's fourth point says it all!

Section 6 — Building Your Career

What does it take to build a successful career in law enforcement? The answer to that has changed in recent years. In the past, good common sense was thought to be the number one attribute necessary for success in policing at any rank. Good common sense is still important, but knowledge of ever-increasingly complex laws, personnel policies, and litigation prevention tactics are all just as necessary.

In the new millennium, progressive and upwardly mobile police officers will reach out and take charge of their careers. They recognize that the minimal training mandated in some states can result in minimal performance, and they want more. They want a successful career with progressively more money, responsibility and prestige. They want a career that serves them well for 20-30 years, and then provides them with a substantial income in their retirement years.

These progressive officers look to a well-balanced career development process to set themselves apart from their peers. They are preparing themselves for success and will be ready when opportunities arise. This balanced approach involves the three keys to success: education, training, and experience, which is a basic guide for any upwardly mobile officer, regardless of their current rank.

Education

As we discussed in Chapter 1, the debate continues as to whether a college-educated officer performs any better on the street than an officer with no college. Although the debate continues, more and more police agencies are requiring some college, and even two- or four-year degrees at entry level.

Formal education can help officers communicate better both orally and in writing—skills that make the jobs of patrolman through chief much easier. Learning about the criminal justice system in an academic environment can also help officers understand their job in context with the many agencies of government. In short, formal education can provide an intellectual framework into which you can put all of your other criminal justice training and experience.

If that isn't enough, look at the common sense aspect of the formal education issue. If your agency requires a two-year degree at entry level, it follows that to supervise these officers and to have credibility with them, perhaps you should have as much or more education than they do. In reality, many departments, formally or informally, are already looking for sergeants with bachelor's degrees, and lieutenants and above with master's degrees.

Your future is up to you on this issue. Spend some of your off-duty hours watching sitcoms on TV, or spend them in a classroom. You can decide for yourself which will pay you better in the future.

Training

"Hey Sarge, I can't go to that DEA school. That's in the middle of hunting season," complains a long-time officer.

"I'll go," volunteers the upwardly mobile officer.

Every training class you go to will help you somehow during your career. Training classes can help you make more and better arrests, understand laws and procedures better, or help save your life. Each class you attend will help you build up your law enforcement résumé, and that can make you better qualified and more confident when being screened, tested, or interviewed for promotions.

And of course, while attending those classes, you will be meeting progressive officers from other precincts, units, or departments. That can be as valuable as the training, because you will repeatedly run into those old friends as you climb the various career ladders in your respective departments. You never know who among your past classmates might be looking for an upwardly mobile person to fill a supervisory position in their unit.

Experience

The amount of experience an officer has is not solely a function of the time they have on the job. The types of experience they gain will vary from individual to individual. In many departments, the length and type of experience you gain is something you can control, at least to some degree.

Working a busy area as a line officer, or as a supervisor, can help you quickly gain valuable experience. It can also help you to learn from the failures and successes of the people you work with in such a busy area. Don't hesitate to get involved and ask questions. Better that you should learn from someone else's mistake than your own.

If you want to move up through the ranks of your department, be sure you get diversified experience. Try not to spend too much time in any particular specialty area. If you want to be a K-9 officer, that's fine. Do it for a few years and move on to some other aspect of the job such as investigations or planning and research. When looking for command-level personnel, top administrators want someone with a diversified background, because those positions often require oversight of several types of units. Overspecialization has been the downfall of many upwardly mobile candidates, particularly when "no suitable replacement" is available for their current highly specialized assignment.

Okay, so you agree that getting your degrees, going to all kinds of training classes, and getting diversified experience is the way to a successful career. Now you ask, "Where do I get the time for all this and still do my job?"

Here is where the common sense answer has to prevail here. First, building a successful career *is* your job. Second, start now. You've got 20 – 30 years to get all the education, training, and experience you can handle. You don't need it all "right away"; you can get it "on your way."

Section 7 — Preparing for Promotion

Preparation is the key to getting promoted.

Even in a highly political environment, competent people must be promoted to key positions to keep the agency running smoothly and without scandal. Senior police commanders look for prepared and competent mid-level commanders who can keep the agency running in a professional manner.

To help you get your "just rewards" in your agency, here are a few tips to help you get promoted:

Start Early

The academy is a good starting place. Establish yourself, early on, as a serious, professional and upwardly mobile candidate at the beginning. Study hard, ask questions and do your best.

A solid foundation is necessary to build anything that can stand the test of time. Start your career with this strong foundation and ignore your less committed critics.

Learn From Others

When one of your fellow officers makes a solid arrest, ask how he or she did it. Their insight will help you to learn how best to do your job.

If they make an arrest for "Burglary 1st," look up the elements of the offense, and the case law relating to that offense, so that you will know how to professionally evaluate and execute an arrest on a similar case of your own in the future. In doing so, you will also improve your chances of correctly answering a question on that offense on your next promotional exam.

Avoid Problems

When police officers around you make mistakes, learn from their mistakes. Avoiding problems in police work requires you to know the law, interpret the law effectively and to do the "right thing."

However, in order to be effective, you must have the education, training, and experience to know what the "right thing" is under the circumstances.

With adequate preparation, and a little forethought, you will seldom have problems in a professional police department at any rank if you do the "right thing."

Be Committed

Your goal is to be the best police officer, sergeant, lieutenant, or chief that you can be. You are to serve the public trust in a professional manner regardless of your current rank.

Keep that focus in your upwardly mobile quest. It will serve you well.

Prepare, Prepare, Prepare

If you receive a new directive on the "Handling of Hazardous Material Spills," read it, learn from it, and put it in your "promotions" file. New directives are often the subject of promotional exam questions or oral interview questions.

Look at other recent, important and controversial operations or personnel issues and try to anticipate questions that could be asked about your understanding and decision making about that current, in vogue, issue. In short, know what's going on, or you will be left behind.

Make Your Intentions Known

If you want to be considered as a serious candidate for promotions, let it be known that you are willing to accept the responsibility of a promotion.

The "will" to command is an historically important component to success in any command position. That willingness to command will show not only your desire, but will also draw attention to your preparation for the position. All that attention will separate you from much of your competition who have less resolve.

Get a Mentor

Sometimes a mentor will find you and help you find your path to success. That is generally because you have shown them your potential for success through your work and the actions previously described.

In some cases you may need to seek the counsel of those successful individuals in your organization who can help you succeed. It's not tough. It may be as simple as, "Captain, I'd like to go up the ranks in this organization. Can you help direct me?"

They will.

Learn the Rules

Many candidates fail to learn the rules for getting promoted, and then wonder why they didn't get promoted.

Study the formula for promotion in your department. Is the emphasis on academics, the written exam, or the oral interview?

If the emphasis is on the academics, or the law, or policies and procedures, then determine where you should concentrate your efforts. If the emphasis in your department is on the oral interview, then you need to concentrate your efforts in that area to be sure you can respond to their questions. This emphasis should be based on your study of your own department's promotional process, which you must research.

Every department has different priorities. Do your homework in this area.

Get the Resources You Need

Up-to-date law books, guides on how to take exams, and advice for maximizing your performance in oral interviews or assessment centers are readily available if you are serious about getting promoted.

With promotions worth thousands of dollars per year, extending into retirement, investing a couple hundred dollars to outpace your competition is an investment in your future as well as your family's future.

Do Your Best

We are not all destined to be the chief of a major department. The majority of police command personnel will never reach the rank of chief or sheriff. That's okay.

The issue at any rank is: "Are you doing the best job you can in your position?" If you can answer "yes" to that question, then your performance speaks for itself. Chances are that those above you will recognize your achievements and want you even higher in their chain of command of successful police leaders.

Your best chance for getting promoted is to be a professional at every rank, prepare for the next rank, and always do the best you can. That bit of advice, and your personal preparation, will serve you well throughout your career wherever it may take you.

Section 8 — Supervisory Ethics

Every profession has a set of ethical standards that its members are expected to follow, and law enforcement is no exception. The Law Enforcement Code of Ethics formulated by the International Association of Chiefs of Police is a general ethical guide for police officers.

However, police supervisors often face dilemmas that are not covered by that particular code of ethics. Rather than facing street-level policing situations, they are much more likely to face personnel problems, promotional considerations, disciplinary actions, and a host of other internal situations. From outside the department, police supervisors face competition for limited funding, community accountability situations, and perceived or actual political pressures.

Although there may not be a specific Police Supervisor's Code of Ethics, asking yourself a few simple questions can help you make correct and ethical decisions throughout your career. So, when faced with making personnel or departmental decisions in that "gray" ethical area, here are a few questions to ask yourself.

Is My Decision Legal?

Although you are sworn to uphold the law, today's supervisory decisions may fall under a set of laws that you didn't learn in the Academy. Personnel decisions must be made carefully and with full knowledge of Title VII's anti-discrimination provisions, the maternity leave acts, the Americans with Disabilities Act and a host of other laws. Other supervisory decisions must conform to Constitutional Law and civil rights laws. A police supervisor must not only know the provisions of the actual laws, but they must also have a working knowledge of all of the associated case law for each provision to avoid making decisions that may not pass legal scrutiny.

Is My Decision Based on Emotion Rather than Facts?

Emotional decisions are seldom good decisions. The negative emotions of anger, revenge, jealousy, lust, or greed must not be allowed to adversely influence the actual facts and circumstances of a dilemma. Other emotional considerations such as compassionate understanding or empathy can be allowed to weigh in for the decision-making process to mitigate the circumstances or motives, but good ethical decisions should be made primarily on the facts.

Is It Worth My Job and/or My Career?

Police supervisors and administrators can be faced with some very difficult ethical decisions. In some cases, extreme outside pressures can be brought to bear from civilian bosses, special interest groups, and politicians—all seeking a favorable decision for their own purposes.

At times such as those, a police supervisor must evaluate the potential consequences of their decision, both pro and con. One single decision can have long-term influence and consequences. The question each individual supervisor must ask himself or herself is, "How far am I willing to go to maintain both my ethics and my job?" Only you know the answer to that question.

Is My Decision Fair to All Concerned?

After gathering all of the facts and circumstances of a given situation, take the time to look at the situation in terms of the people involved in it. If you choose to discipline a particular employee, is your action fair to them? On the other hand, would your failure to take disciplinary action be fair to others who do their best to follow the rules and avoid such disciplinary actions.

Law enforcement supervision, like street work is still a person-to-person business and it will remain so. Taking the time to evaluate the situation in human terms can help you make better ethical decisions. With fundamental fairness as the cornerstone of your decision-making process, you can better evaluate the totality of the situation and make sound and ethical decisions.

Last and perhaps the most important question to ask yourself is:

Is it the Right Thing to Do?

So many factors go into making the right decision that you cannot consciously evaluate each individual factor and its effect or your decision-making process. This is the time to take a deep breath and let your intuition take over for a moment. Do you have an uneasy feeling about making a particular decision? Then there is something wrong with it. On the other hand if a particular decision intuitively "feels good," then it is probably the right decision to make.

As you progress in your career, you will often be faced with ethical dilemmas both small and large. How you respond to those challenges will determine who you are and how you are perceived by others, both inside and outside the department. It is your choice as to whether you are perceived as a competent and ethical police commander, or as something else.

In your daily activities, as well as in those difficult dilemmas, rely on your years of law enforcement education, training, and experience. In difficult situations, stop and ask yourself the five preceding questions. Then make your best decision.

Chances are, you'll be doing the right thing!

Chapter 3
YOU GOT PROMOTED — NOW WHAT?

By working faithfully eight hours a day, you may eventually get to be a boss and work twelve hours a day.

— Robert Frost

Section 1 — Are You a Positive Role Model?

Section 2 — Decision Time!

Section 3 — Maintaining Standards

Section 4 — Good Communications

Section 5 — Handling Mistakes

Section 6 — Do You Recognize Good Work?

Section 7 — Supervisory Notifications

Section 8 — Managerial Mistakes to Avoid

Lt Cap – middle management.
Sergeant – line level.

Section 1 — Are You a Positive Role Model?

As a police administrator and supervisor, you routinely make decisions, solve problems, and generally run your department on a daily basis. However, as you go about your various duties, are you aware that your employees are watching everything you do, and the way you do it?

What kind of an effect are the actions they observe having on your people? More than you may realize!

First, as a supervisor at any rank, you are a role model for those who are coming up through the ranks. Their observations of your daily routine and actions may be the only frame of reference they have as to how a person of your rank should perform. When they get promoted, they will naturally assume that they should act the same way you did—good or bad!

Second, as the person in charge, your people look to you for guidance, and as a source of power. They also will tend to emulate your attitudes, your demeanor, and even your appearance—good, or bad!

For these reasons, you are in a position to be a positive, competent and professional role model. Or, you can represent everything that is wrong with the promotional system in your department.

It's all up to you!

To help you to be that positive role model, here are 10 DOs and 10 DON'Ts for you to follow. How do you stack up?

make note card

DO:	DON'T:
• Look Like a Professional	• Be Closed-Minded
• Maintain a Positive Attitude	• Be Two-Faced
• Be Fair	• Gossip
• Be Honest	• Complain
• Be Available	• Be Lazy
• Make Timely Decisions	• Be Arrogant
• Recognize Good Work	• Over Manage
• Be Consistent	• Hold Grudges
• Be Knowledgeable, and	• Criticize in Public, or
• Respect Your Employees	• Be Insensitive

In short, be a model employee, maintain high standards, and others will pattern themselves after you. That's good for them, for you, and for the department.

Section 2 — Decision Time!

How many times a day does someone start a conversation with you by asking "Can I…?" "Should I…?," or by starting with words such as "Who?" "What?" or "When?" As a supervisor, you probably hear them several times a day, every day. And, chances are that in each case, you are required to make some type of decision before you are able to answer them back.

The fact is that being a supervisor at any level *requires* that you have the ability to make decisions. In order for you to be successful, each decision you make must be sound, timely, and based on the facts and circumstances of the particular situation at hand.

Supervisors who consistently make such valid decisions know that the secret to their success is found in using a logical, multi-stage, decision-making process. This process, when properly followed, and combined with a little common sense, will lead any supervisor down the path to success.

Although some decisions are made in seconds, some in minutes, and some in days, they are all made the same way. Here is the procedure:

Gather the Facts

Just as in a criminal investigation, information is the key. You need to understand the whole situation. Therefore, you need to collect all of the facts and circumstances you can in a reasonable amount of time.

Analyze Those Facts

Review all of the information objectively. You must be able to clearly see the entire situation and who is affected by it. Be confident that you have a good grasp of the situation.

Formulate Possible Decisions

Think of all the possible decisions you could make. Then consider the consequences of each one on the people and circumstances involved. Consider both the short-term and the long-term effects.

Choose the Best One — Then Implement It!

Be prepared to stand behind your decision. Ensure that you will be able to articulate your reasons for making that particular decision. If called upon to explain your actions, do so in a forthright and confident manner, citing your reasons. You will seldom be called wrong.

Knorr Even though you should be prepared to defend your actions, continue to keep an open mind. If new facts become known, or if circumstances suddenly change, you are perfectly justified in modifying your original decision to meet the changing environment.

Knorr If you are to gain the trust and respect of your subordinates and superiors, you must be able to consistently make sound and timely decisions. Following the hints outlined here should help you toward that goal.

Section 3 — Maintaining Standards

In general, law enforcement supervisors get into trouble for what they don't do. The duties and responsibilities of a law enforcement supervisor, at any level, are so numerous and diverse that it can be easy to overlook something.

And the one thing that you overlook is the one that will get you and your department on the 6 o'clock news, and put your career on shaky ground.

One of your responsibilities as a supervisor or commander is to maintain the standards that are set for your people and your department. In some departments, the standards are set high originally, but then those high standards erode over time, due to tolerance or lack of due vigilance by command personnel. Sometimes these lowered standards can explode in short order, such as in a front-page case of police brutality. Other times, a slow erosion of professional standards eventually ends up in unprofessional conduct and public disdain for the department and its members. And, the leadership of the police department, at all levels, is to blame for such a failure.

To protect yourself, your career, your people, and your department, here are a few tips to help you take an inventory of your current standards and your responsibility to maintain them.

1. Quality of Work

Whether the work that you oversee consists of routine reports or the accounting of department funds, you have a right to expect good work by your people. They are being paid taxpayer dollars to do the job, and it should be done properly. It is your responsibility to ensure that your people comply with standard policies, procedures, and general operating practices. Those who choose to be sloppy, lazy or just inept, must be taken to task, and the job must be done right before you accept it.

Quantity of Work

Setting performance standards for the quantity of work can be difficult, particularly when setting standards at the street level. Avoiding allegations of "quota setting," and the politics of that allegation can be challenging but not insurmountable for a professional police commander. What can be done is to set the quantity of work to be done, by anyone in the organization, at a reasonable level obtainable through reasonable effort for the area in which they work. A detailed productivity study can help, but you probably already have all the information you need. After all, you were there, and you know what it takes to do the job. You have been "there," and can insist on a reasonable quantity of work for the bucks they are being paid.

Safety

Yes, law enforcement work is a dangerous job. But it becomes less dangerous when supervisors run their operations with safety in mind. Be sure that you have adequate people, equipment, and backup before placing your people in harm's way. Control the situation to prevent bravado courage or poor execution. Plan ahead, train your people well, and maintain on-scene discipline, at all ranks. You will be required to place your people in harm's way occasionally, but don't ever do it needlessly.

Grooming

It is just plain fact. If police officers look like professional police officers, the public will respect them as professionals. And, the converse is true. If they look sloppy, wrinkled, and have "customized" their appearance to their own liking, despite the department's rules and regulations, the public will respect them much less. That lack of respect will cause them problems on the street, and their problems will become your problems through injured prisoners, citizen complaints, etc. A simple, "Get those shoes shined before you hit the street," can prevent a lot of problems for everybody.

Ethics

A 1,500-page policy and procedures manual is a good step toward a professional police department, but any one of those rules can be bent, broken, or ignored. The antidote for unethical, unprofessional, or illegal behavior is proper supervision, management, and leadership. And that would be your job, at whatever level that you command. Insisting that your police officers always—and we mean always—try to do "the right thing," in every facet of their work, and at every level, is your job. Tough? You bet! But, it's your duty and responsibility.

So what do they call law enforcement units or departments that demand a reasonable quality and quantity of work from their members; watch out for the safety of its people, as well as demand high grooming and ethical standards from its officers?

Professional!

And what do they call the law enforcement commanders of these units or departments?

Leaders!

What do they call unprofessional law enforcement officers, units, and departments behind their backs?

You don't want to find out!

Section 4 — Good Communications

Communication, at any level, is an inexact art. Misunderstood communications are a problem in any industry, but the problems have far greater consequences in the life and death world of law enforcement.

With the lives of civilians and officers on the line, law enforcement commanders need to have the best communication skills they can develop to avert future tragedies.

Here are a few tips for enhancing your communication skills, both in the office, and on the street.

"You Talkin' Ta Me?"

Whether you are speaking or writing, use words and phrases that your audience understands. There is a big difference between talking to an angry crowd of sports fans and giving a planning presentation to your executive board. One group might see your big words and perfect articulation as a strength; the other as a weakness. Know the difference, and adapt accordingly.

Always be sure to speak and write in terms of the education, maturity level, and experience of the recipient of the communication.

Ask for Input

Good commanders at all levels recognize that they can't know everything about every situation. Therefore, as a part of their communication process, they ask for the input of others. They consider the information, views, and opinions of others, including subordinates, peers, superiors, and other outside sources, including the public.

The key to good decision-making is gathering the facts, at the proper time and place, and in the proper sequence to evaluate them and their consequences. Therefore, you can't make your best decisions without asking for the input of others.

Be Clear and Concise

In verbal or written communications, simpler is better. First, think about what you want to say. Then think about the simplest way to say it. Make notes of the key points. Then prepare your thoughts for presentation.

Avoid excessive background material or rambling. Get to the point! Explain, clearly and concisely, what needs to be done, when, and, in some cases, how.

Let each individual communique deal with a simple action or objective. Including requests for multiple actions will confuse some people, and may cause some issues or actions to be lost in the process.

Be clear, concise, and to the point about what you want done and when to do it.

Get Feedback

Were your orders or directives understood? You will never know until your project or objective either succeeds or fails, unless you ask questions and get feedback about your original orders.

You knew what you wanted done, you spent time to communicate your wishes to others, but what did they really hear?

Ask them. "Officer Jones, what is your understanding of my directive?" is a good start. Spot-check to be sure that your people really heard what you meant, and that they will proceed in the proper direction with your orders.

Communication is such an inexact art that to have someone provide you with their express understanding of your words is critical in any verbal or written communication.

Follow-Up

Even though you followed all of the preceding steps, and you felt confident that everyone understood your oral or written communication, successful commanders take the next step and follow up on their orders. Your orders may have been clear and concise to the receiver, but typically those orders are passed from level-to-level and person-to-person within your organization.

Seldom are the people who directly received your orders the ones who actually implement those orders. And, given the inexact nature of communications, your orders can get distorted in the process. Somehow in the process, your directive to "curtail all unnecessary non-patrol activities to conserve gas," became "stop all patrol activities" to conserve gas—a missed and critical communication gap.

Successful commanders recognize the problems of the interpretation of words and phrases, and that individuals will hear, read, and interpret those words consistent with their own values, views, and agendas. Recognizing that, and other factors, successful commanders take the steps necessary to prevent "communication problems" from getting out of hand.

So remember, whether you are dealing with a tough street sweep or the executive board, the phrase "We are moving forward!" can have far different meanings and consequences to each of the recipients.

Section 5 — Handling Mistakes

It starts out innocently, "Boss, you got a minute?" Whether you do or not, your subordinate proceeds to tell you about the mistake he made, thereby dropping the whole thing right into your lap. Now what?

Mistakes are a fact of life. Your subordinates will make them, and occasionally you will make them as well. The success of your career may depend on your ability to handle mistakes, avoidable or not, whenever they occur.

Here are a few hints to help you handle mistakes, and the problems they can create.

Evaluate It!

Acknowledge that a mistake has occurred, keeping in mind that all mistakes can be handled. Stay calm, and realistically evaluate how much damage has been done. When you think through it logically, chances are there is less damage than originally appeared.

Be Up Front

Accept responsibility for the mistake and advise your supervisor of the situation. You may also need to advise anyone else who will be directly affected by it as well. However, that's about it! There is no sense in broadcasting a mistake to the entire organization if it's not necessary.

Handle It

Formulate, then act on, a plan of action to correct the mistake and to minimize the effect of it. Take the steps necessary to ensure that it doesn't happen again. Keep your supervisor informed of your progress as you logically work your way through the entire situation.

Document Your Actions

Record all of the details of the incident: How it occurred, when and how you learned of it, who you notified, and what actions you took. This documentation will be of great value if you have to answer questions at a later date. It will also tend to protect you, your subordinates, and the organization by documenting the events at the time they occur.

Learn and Grow

Experience is a great teacher. The problems and mistakes that you handle will increase your levels of knowledge, maturity, and confidence. At the same time, your ability to effectively handle the situation will be watched by subordinates, and they will learn from your example.

When you handle problems and mistakes calmly, logically, and professionally, you will gain the respect of your subordinates and your superiors. This respect, coupled with the knowledge and experience you gained, should make you a prime candidate when it comes to future promotions.

Section 6 — Do You Recognize Good Work?

While on a security post, Officer Don McCormack heard an unusual noise. He investigated, using all of his senses and previously taught skills. As a result of his stealthy approach and alertness, he apprehended an individual attempting to infiltrate a highly restricted area without incident. He turned that individual over to the investigative personnel and it was determined that, in fact, that individual was a terrorist attempting to infiltrate the secure facility he was assigned to protect.

Officer McCormack didn't hear anything else about the case until about two weeks later at roll call. Sergeant Moore announced that McCormack was to testify the next afternoon before a grand jury regarding the intruder case. "You'll be off your post for about four hours, McCormack," the sergeant announced in a nasty tone. Officer McCormack left roll call confused. He was confused because he knew he had done good work, but apparently nobody cared what he did as long as he was a body available for the next shift's coverage.

Apparently, Sergeant Moore had not heard about the major survey that found that workers repeatedly cited "Full Appreciation for Work Done" as their number one priority for job satisfaction in the workplace. Perhaps he also missed the classes in his supervisory training school that dealt with employee morale, motivation, and interpersonal communications, just to name a few.

Knowledgeable supervisors know that employees respond directly to the feedback they get about their work. They will respond positively to positive feedback about their work and will work even harder when they know their efforts are appreciated. However, when they receive negative feedback, as in the example above, they are most likely to slow down, do just enough to get by, and avoid any contact with their supervisor unless absolutely necessary.

With this in mind, the best supervisors, at any rank, are those who use positive feedback to help their people respond and produce at above-average levels of performance. Those motivated individuals will also continue their excellent performance over time, with a high level of personal job satisfaction and enthusiasm.

In the case cited above, Sergeant Moore should have taken a much more positive view of McCormack's court appearance. He could have made an announcement about the excellent investigation, and he could have joked in a positive way about the possibility of McCormack's "Carrying an investigator's badge the next time we see him."

The sergeant could easily have covered McCormack's shift for four hours. He had done it before for a lot less reason. Instead of viewing it as a break for the officer, and an opportunity for him to learn and grow, Sergeant Moore chose to provide negative feedback to the entire shift. The effects of that negative feedback will probably last a long time.

Regardless of your position within an agency, you can usually turn any situation into an opportunity to provide positive feedback to your subordinates. All you need to do is think about how to do it. Here are a few examples of what can be done to reward employees, make them feel good about themselves and show them that you appreciate the work that they do.

Recognition

When your subordinates are out facing the same tough situations every day, they may feel like they are fighting a fruitless and never-ending battle. Such negative feelings can quickly lead to burnout and job dissatisfaction, particularly when they think nobody really cares about what they are doing.

Take the time to say "thank you" for an employee's continuing efforts to maintain the integrity of the department. Point out the positive impact his investigations have had in protecting the public, object, or facility through excellent alertness, investigations, and documentation of the facts. Your words will help him to view his job in the proper perspective, and will let him know that his efforts are worthwhile and appreciated.

Opportunity for Development

Officer Larry Jones showed an exceptional interest in tactical operations. He read up on them on his own, and was one of the few officers who really knew how important tactical training was to the ultimate success of critical operations.

Sent to the scene of a critical incident as backup, Officer Jones found himself closer to the action than was planned. However, he performed calmly and professionally throughout the difficult and sensitive incident. He had proved that he could handle the stress of a critical situation.

In addition to a positive recommendation for future promotion, his superiors arranged for him to attend a special tactics school for two weeks so he could qualify for a permanent backup position on the Special Tactics Team. Only longer-term veterans had been sent in the past.

Providing Interesting Work

When reviewing the dispatch log, a sergeant noticed that a young officer was taking more than the usual time when handling routine prowler calls at the secure housing area he patrolled. Curious, he responded with the young officer to such a call and found the reason for the extended time.

The young officer, in addition to checking for a prowler, was spending the time to show the resident how to best secure their windows and doors so they would feel safer and to deter future prowlers. In addition, the sergeant found out that the young officer followed up each call to be sure the residents had implemented some of the precautions he recommended.

When the captain announced that he needed someone knowledgeable about crime prevention to address a newly arrived group of residents, the sergeant knew just the right officer to assign. The young officer became the department's resident crime prevention specialist and ultimately became their full-time crime prevention officer.

Whether you are protecting residential facilities, the general public, or dignitaries, you still need to recognize and appreciate the good work of your people. It's not hard. Just look at what they do, stop and think about it, and you will find plenty of reasons to praise their good work, and help them develop a positive future with your organization.

Section 7 — Supervisory Notifications

Law enforcement supervisors and managers cannot work twenty-four hours a day, seven days a week. Yet their commands keep up that ongoing pace relentlessly. How can you reconcile the responsibility of command with the realities of the working world, a family, and a life?

The answer is in the "exception" principle of management. Essentially, that means that each rank should handle only situations that their subordinate officers have neither the authority nor the capacity to handle. If it is a situation that they cannot handle, or they have handled it but it may have further implications, then a superior officer needs to be notified, either for future guidance, a critical decision or just so they know what is going on. In many cases that means calling the superior officer at home to make the notification.

Good commanders, at any rank, provide their people with a set of guidelines for making such supervisory notifications. Put in the form of a memorandum, these guidelines should be provided to each subordinate officer as well as posted in an appropriate place in the department for handy reference during critical incidents. Here is a list of incidents that a law enforcement supervisor or manager might provide to his/her people for them to make appropriate supervisory notifications.

Serious Injuries to Any Officer or Employee

Every police supervisor should have a great concern for his/her subordinates' welfare. If an officer is seriously injured, the commander of that unit should be notified immediately so he/she can take appropriate action on the care of the officer or employee, as well as making additional supervisory notifications.

Use-of-Force Incidents Involving Serious Injury or Death to a Civilian or a Suspect

The nature of law enforcement work is such that the police will occasionally be required to use force, even deadly physical force, against civilian suspects. When serious injury or death occurs as a result of such police actions, the commander of the unit should be notified to ensure that all appropriate steps are taken to document the circumstances of the incident for the protection of all persons involved in the incident.

Incidents Involving Police Officers of Other Jurisdictions

Occasionally, incidents will occur that involve officers of other jurisdictions operating within the geographic boundaries assigned to a particular police commander. Such actions are common in the case of multi-jurisdictional task forces and federal or state law enforcement units operating within local jurisdictions. Proper and timely supervisory notifications of such incidents can prevent jurisdictional or "turf" problems from flaring up at a later time.

Incidents Involving Off-Duty Police Officers

Whether they are officers of your own or of another jurisdiction, any unusual or unlawful conduct by off-duty officers should result in the immediate notification, through channels, to the commander of the jurisdiction where the incident occurred. This timely notification will allow the commander to communicate with the errant officer's commander to determine the appropriate actions to be taken by each jurisdiction in the matter.

Serious Crimes

Although the term "serious crime" can vary from jurisdiction to jurisdiction, some specific guidelines may be necessary to be sure that only appropriate supervisory notifications are made. The seizure of a kilo of cocaine may be big news in a small suburban town, but not a cause for immediate supervisory notification in some cities, where it is an all-too-routine occurrence for an immediate supervisory notification.

Incidents Involving Prominent Public Figures

From politicians to rock stars, the interest generated by police involvement with these high profile people will become a highly publicized event. With the proper supervisory notifications made in a timely manner, the police commander can mobilize the appropriate resources necessary to handle the media onslaught that can follow such high-profile incidents.

Incidents Involving Media-Sensitive Issues

There may be local or national media coverage of selected events, issues, or persons. Such situations can include many "hot button" issues that are often controversial. Prompt supervisory notifications when such incidents occur will allow police commanders to be prepared for the media and political ramifications of the incident, rather than be caught unaware and short-handed.

Any Other Incident or Arrest of an Unusual or Highly Controversial Nature

This catchall phrase allows subordinate commanders to have the latitude to call upon a commander at their own discretion, whether for immediate guidance, for future planning, or just because they are not sure exactly what they should do in a particular situation.

The responsibility of a command, of a squad, a unit, or a department is a difficult and demanding task. It is not a 9 to 5 responsibility. In order to perform effectively, law enforcement commanders must be kept apprised of critical incidents when they occur.

Conversely, subordinate commanders need definitive guidelines to follow to ensure that their commanders receive timely notification of such critical incidents without being notified of relatively trivial events that could wait until the commander comes back on duty.

The issue here is effective communications both up and down the chain of command. You can help foster such good and effective communications by writing that memorandum setting out the foregoing supervisory notification guidelines, as well as your own thoughts on the matter. You will be helping yourself as well as those young officers who often ask themselves, "Should I call the boss on this one or not?"

Section 8 — Managerial Mistakes to Avoid

When a group of incumbent police managers was asked to prepare a list of the management mistakes they had made in their careers, they could think of none.

When the same group was asked to prepare a list of management mistakes that they had seen *others* make, they had no problem making a substantial list.

From that second list, here are the six most serious management mistakes that you and your other management personnel should try to avoid, especially when first taking over a new unit or command.

Indecision

In an industry that deals with public safety, and where seconds can make the difference between a successful police action or a disaster, it's no wonder that indecision is on this list of management mistakes. The process of making sound and timely decisions is a learnable skill for most people. Therefore, there is no excuse for a police commander, at any rank, to be guilty of indecision.

Failure to Motivate Subordinates

When subordinates fail to meet a police commander's expectations, he/she tries to motivate the individual members who are under-performing within the unit. This can work if the unmotivated officers are a small percentage of the unit.

But, if the whole unit, or a substantial portion of the unit is under-performing reasonable expectations, then the culprit is a lack of leadership from the current commander of that unit. Leadership is the ability to know what your unit should be doing, understanding what it takes to get them there, and developing a commitment from your unit that they will follow your lead. That type of dynamic leadership inspires the effective motivation of your people.

Failure to Give Positive Reinforcement

The very nature of police work requires officers to catch people doing something wrong. After years of this behavior on the street, officers are promoted, take over a unit, and catch their own people—doing something wrong.

Police commanders at all ranks need to overcome their pasts if they are to avoid this managerial mistake. Your people want to be commended for exceptional work, as well as simply being recognized for doing everyday work well. Take the time out of your busy day to catch some of your people—doing something right.

The next three managerial mistakes are all interrelated, and are very common mistakes made by both new, and experienced, police commanders. Try to avoid all of them, individually and collectively.

Failure to Solicit Input from Subordinates

It is a foolish commander who thinks he/she can know everything and make a perfect decision every time. Your people have information that can help you make a better decision in a given situation. They can also help you foresee any problems down the road when you select one option over another.

Couple the advantages of enhancing your decision-making capability with the fact that your subordinates want some degree of control over their own destiny. They want their voices heard and their opinions valued. Even if the final decision doesn't go their way, they will feel some ownership of the process and satisfaction at having had the opportunity to be heard.

Coming on Too Strong

It is true that when taking over a new unit, it is better to come on a little too strong than a little too weak. The supporting theory is that it will be much easier to "back off" a little once your authority is established than it is to retake any position that your weakness gave up.

So how strong is too strong? As the new commander, you need to evaluate the unit's mission, performance, and personalities. You also need to lead, consistent with your own personality. You are the one who must make the decision on how strong is too strong. That's why you are the commander.

Being Too Autocratic

It is quite possible to be a strong leader without being perceived as autocratic. Professional commanders work on their "people skills" as well as their "technical skills." There are times when you must, as a police commander, lean toward the autocratic, but most of the time you can operate in a subordinate friendly and approachable manner.

You should treat your people with dignity and respect and seek their input on both important and small matters. When you care about the safety and security of your people, it is hard to be thought of as autocratic. You are much more likely to be perceived as a strong and caring leader of your unit.

Rest assured that you will occasionally make a managerial mistake; just try not to make any of the six that we just listed.

Chapter 4
GAINING CONFIDENCE

Believe in yourself! Have faith in your abilities! Without a humble, but reasonable confidence in your own powers, you cannot be successful or happy.

— Norman Vincent Peale

Section 1 — Confidence is Critical!

Your subordinates must have confidence in your ability to be their leader if you are to be an effective commander. The question is how do you gain that confidence.

Here are a few tips that may help you.

Appear Confident

In a world where appearances are as important as realities, you must appear confident and in charge at the scene of any incident. Your calm air of confidence will come naturally if you understand your role, have the background and knowledge to do the job, and the fortitude to be ready and able to do what is necessary to get the job hone.

To reach that point, you need to prepare, prepare, and prepare. Study and learn every aspect of your job from the case law to the tactics. Mentally prepare to be the commander of a scene, capable of balancing the need to get the job done with watching out for the welfare of your people. Know your own strengths and weaknesses, as well as the capabilities of your unit.

Once physically and mentally prepared, you will automatically exude a self-confidence that will be recognized by your subordinates. They will then be willing to follow your lead in any crisis.

Encourage Free Speech

Your subordinates also have a great deal of knowledge and experience in law enforcement. Allow them to share that knowledge and experience with you. Solicit their opinions and ideas. *"What would you do if you were in my position?"* This question, asked with sincerity and confidence, will elicit perspectives and ideas you may not have considered.

Even if you have to make a final decision that is not in agreement with the counsel of your subordinates, at least they had the opportunity to express their opinions on the matter at hand. Thank them for their input and explain that because you are the one who must take the ultimate responsibility, you must make the final decision as you see it, taking into account all of the information you have received from them and other sources. Your subordinates, even those who may not agree with your decision, will respect you for your ability to make the decision and go forward.

Keep Your People Informed

Officers are accustomed to gathering facts, making their own decisions based on those facts, and thereby controlling their own destiny. If you take away their ability to gather solid facts, the rumor mill fills the void and officers will use those rumors in place of facts to speculate about their destinies.

Good commanders realize that there is very little in policing that requires great secrecy. They keep their subordinates as informed as possible. When rumors surface, a good commander tracks them down and replaces them with the facts of the matter.

As a result, subordinates learn to go to the commander to get the "straight scoop" on any issue. The trust that this builds up over time substantially increases their confidence in their commander.

Keep Promises

Although it seems like common sense, too many supervisors fail to keep promises made to their subordinates. They don't do it intentionally, they just promise too much, without having the authority or ability to deliver on the promise. When that happens, the confidence level of subordinates drops dramatically.

Experienced commanders know better than to make promises they can't keep. They can promise to try to get an unpopular policy changed, but they know that they can't change it themselves. They can only take their concerns to the policy makers and try to be influential enough to get the policy changed. Whether they are successful or not, they have kept their promise by trying to get it changed.

To garner the confidence of your employees, keep your promises, or don't make them.

Remove Unnecessary Roadblocks

Your employees will become frustrated with impediments to getting their work done and it is up to you to clear the way for them to do their work.

As an example, in your city, the precinct captain must approve the execution of all search warrants in the precinct. A search warrant has just been issued, but the precinct captain is at a wedding. Your officers are frustrated and fear destruction of important evidence if they don't get approval in a short period of time. It is up to you to get the approval, as unobtrusively as possible, but get the approval, so your officers can move forward.

Over time, when you have shown your people that you know what you are doing, you listen to them, keep them informed, and you can get things done, your people will learn to trust you and to have confidence in you. Once that happens you will know it when the senior man in your unit asks: "Sarge, what do you want us to do next?"

Section 2 — "Commander, You Got a Minute?"

When you claim the title of "commander" of any type of unit, you tacitly agree to make yourself available whenever your people need you. Those who report to you will often need your guidance, support, or perhaps just a quick decision during a critical incident.

It is up to you to ensure that your actions and attitudes convey your willingness to meet their needs and your obligations. To assist in preparing yourself and your people, here are a few hints on how to be available, and accessible, when your people need you.

Be Dependable

Your subordinates need to be able to find you quickly when they need you. In the often fast-paced world of law enforcement, a delay in getting a critical decision, or a lack of timely guidance from a supervisor, can allow a situation to escalate far beyond where it should have been controlled.

Therefore, you should always make arrangements so that you can be reached quickly, either in person, by telephone, radio, or beeper. Depending on your actual rank and position, this can mean off-duty, as well as on-duty. As long as subordinates know that they can depend on reaching you, they will be more willing to seek your guidance in critical situations. That willingness alone can be a key factor in keeping a particular mission or project from getting out of hand.

Be Friendly and Approachable

Although being available is very important, it is also important that you put yourself in a position where subordinates are willing to approach you. Studies have repeatedly shown that the supervisor who is open and friendly with subordinates has the greatest chance of success. Keeping that in mind, be sure that you take the initiative in talking with your people and getting to know them. In doing so, you will also be helping them get to know you, and that will help them to become comfortable talking with you.

Keep your office door open. Encourage them to ask you questions and make it clear that their inquiries are welcomed. Maintaining such a positive atmosphere will ensure that there is no hesitation in contacting you when a critical situation occurs. You will be kept informed, and they will be assured that their actions are appropriate as a result of your guidance.

Take Your Time

When a subordinate asks for assistance, be sure to thoroughly address their needs. Make their problem your number one priority until it is resolved to their satisfaction. Take as much time as is needed.

Whether it involves a quick decision, or a lengthy explanation of a new policy, the time spent will be a good investment. That's because when a similar situation occurs in the future, the thorough explanation or action you previously took will allow the subordinate to handle the situation without your assistance. That way, the employee grows, and you are free to concentrate on other duties, knowing that you have a capable subordinate handling the situation.

Showing that you are approachable and willing to share your expertise and experience with your people will help build the element of trust in your relationships with them. The advantage to them is that they will feel more secure in their work, knowing that you are there if they need you. The advantage to you is that you will know that they will contact you for input if they feel it is necessary.

Making yourself readily available, approachable, and willing to help your subordinates can help ensure the success of a mission or project that is your responsibility. Therefore, the next time you hear "Commander, you got a minute?" consider it a tribute to your management skills and a form of job security.

Section 3 — Handle It!

Law enforcement at any level requires an ability to confront and handle situations, problems, and conflicts. The decision making and problem solving for every situation should be made at the lowest possible level in the police organization. If the sergeant can "handle it," then he should. If not, it should go to the lieutenant to be handled, and so on.

Taking care of problems at the lowest possible level serves several very valuable functions in the department. First, it frees up upper-level command officers to better perform their primary duties of acquiring the necessary resources (money, political support, etc.) to run the department. It also allows upper-level commanders to perform strategic planning, allocate resources, create and manage the budget, and so on.

For the lower-level commanders, usually sergeants and lieutenants, who must make the decisions and solve the problems, there are also several advantages. First, they gain valuable experience in handling difficult situations that will help them prepare for future command-level positions. Their commanders also will be observing their performances and evaluating their future promotability. Although both of these factors are important, the satisfaction and confidence gained in handling a different or complex situation, without needing help, is a valuable confidence builder.

To help officers better "handle it" when the time comes, here are a few practical tips.

Follow the Guidelines

Many commanders have confronted situations similar to those you will face. From their experiences, your department's policy and procedure manual has evolved. Become familiar with it, before you are confronted with a difficult situation. However, even though it has grown over the years, realize that it may not cover everything.

Know Your Capabilities

To effectively handle numerous situations, you must be able to deploy the correct combination of patrol, investigative and specialized personnel, and equipment. Therefore, you must know what resources you have, where they are located, and the process you need to follow to access them in a timely manner to prevent situations from escalating to the next level.

Make a Plan

For some major incidents, such as natural disasters (hurricanes, floods, etc.), your department most likely has a disaster plan in place. If so, you need to review it so you can begin to implement it at the earliest possible times. For lesser situations, mostly man-made, you will need to formulate a plan. That plan may be a mini-version of the bigger disaster plan. Making a plan, with your past knowledge, will help you solve the critical situations that you face.

Take the Risk

Although there are no guarantees of success in critical situations, you are a knowledgeable and prepared commander. You will have a "feel" for what it takes to solve the situation. Implementing your original plan, with the proper manpower and resources at the right time, requires an element of risk, but it will be with a "reasonable expectation of winning." To delay could make matters worse. A word of caution—always have a withdrawal strategy and a backup plan, with additional help on its way before committing your personnel.

Accept the Responsibility

As the highest ranking person at the scene of a critical incident, it is up to you to "handle it" until you are relieved. You should accept this responsibility for the good of your people, your department, and your community. Yes, you need to advise your immediate supervisor of the current situation, and help may be on its way, but it is you who have to make the critical decisions and take the proper actions for now.

Do the Right Thing

The department has given you guidelines, you know the laws that govern your actions and you have your past law enforcement experiences to draw from. But there is no substitute for listening to your internal physical, mental, and moral self that tells you the actions you are about to take are the "right thing to do" for the situation you are facing.

By following your policies, procedures, and other guidelines listed above, you should be well on your way to properly handling the situation you are facing. If you continually follow that course of action, it is likely to take you up the ladder of success within your department.

Section 4 — Managing Change

Change is inevitable in any organization! Departmental goals, policies, and procedures are always subject to change. As a ranking officer, it is your responsibility to take the initiative and implement those changes in a smooth and efficient manner. To do this, you must manage the change process from beginning to end.

Following a few simple rules can help make your job, and the jobs of your subordinates, much easier during this change process. The effective implementation of change in your unit will reflect very favorably on your performance as a commander. Supervisors who fail to effectively manage the change process run the risk of seriously damaging their careers.

Prepare for the Change

Few changes are thrust on you with absolutely no warning. A good supervisor stays alert to future change possibilities and begins managing the process immediately. By monitoring recent court decisions, unusual local cases, and nationally publicized incidents, you can gain valuable insight into what changes may soon occur in your department. Begin by discussing the subject or case casually with your employees. Gauge their reactions to some of the changes that could be brought about as a result of what has occurred. Allow them to vent their ideas and feelings on the subject. Listen to them carefully. Before the hint of change arrives on your department's doorstep, you will have already identified problem areas, explored various options, as well as having identified the employees who may resist certain changes, and those who are willing to readily accept certain changes.

Keep Everyone Informed

Begin a dialogue with all who could be affected by changes in the area under consideration. If you find extreme resistance to a particular alternative from your employees during your informal discussions, convey those concerns to your boss. If you sense strong feelings toward a particular alternative from your boss, convey that to your employees to help them prepare for that possible alternative. Such open communication can help to reach a compromise acceptable to everyone in the organization and can lead to an extremely smooth transition. Naturally, you must be careful during this procedure to ensure that you don't violate anyone's confidence, up or down the chain of command.

Be Honest and Straightforward

If you are a good supervisor, your opinion on the matter under consideration will be valued by both your subordinates and superiors alike. If you are a respected and informed member of the management team, your honest and knowledgeable opinion can make a difference. This is not the time to be quiet, because you will be living with the final changes as much as anyone else. Make your feelings known on the matter, but keep a flexible stance. You may have to ultimately implement a decision substantially different from the one you originally favored. Even if that occurs, you will have gained respect from everyone for making your feelings known in a knowledgeable and professional manner.

Explain and "Sell"

When the decisions have been made at levels above your rank, it is finally time to explain the new policy or procedure to your employees, often at a group meeting. Try to explain why the decision was made and why it was viewed as the best alternative. Focus on the factors that will affect your people personally. Also help them to see how the change will favorably affect the department's mission. Allow reasonable discussions on the matter and respond to all concerns. Assure them that you will personally support the decision, and that you expect it to be implemented as quickly and as smoothly as possible. It is a major part of your job as a police supervisor to "sell" the decisions of your superiors, whether or not you agree with them.

Avoid Overkill

When explaining the changes to your subordinates, not everyone will readily accept them despite your best efforts. When you feel that the subject has been fully presented and discussed, and that a large majority of the employees will accept the changes, end the meeting. If you feel it is necessary to continue discussions, meet any particular employee one-on-one in your office. Further discussion may be worthwhile, but eventually the discussion must end and you must make it clear that the appropriate changes must be implemented by all employees, whether they personally agree with them or not.

Caution

Because it is a part of your job on the "management team" to implement upper-level decisions, be sure that you do so honestly. If you do not convey the impression that you personally support the decision and that you seriously intend to see this change implemented, your people will not take the change seriously and will tend to ignore it. That will lead to problems within the unit and will ultimately cause problems and conflict up and down the chain of command. You will become the person in the middle and the resulting turmoil will undermine your authority. In addition, you will be seen as an ineffective leader when your people don't implement the directed changes.

Change will continue to occur in the field of law enforcement just as it does in the rest of the world. Those who accept the necessary changes and manage the change process effectively will continue to be successful commanders. Those who can't, or won't, accept change, will find themselves with chronic problems within their units. Ultimately those ineffective commanders will be removed from their units and be replaced by someone who can effectively manage the inevitable change process.

Section 5 — Handling Controversy

The ability to handle controversy is critical to the success of any police commander at any rank. The problem may be internal to your department, such as a disagreement over who is getting promoted or allegations of selective discipline. Or the controversy may involve disagreements over external issues such as police policies or tactics and how they are implemented in your community.

Because handling controversy is such a critical skill, here are a few tips to help you handle it.

Controversy is Inevitable

Understanding that controversy is a part of your environment, and accepting the fact that you must handle it, puts you in a good position to effectively handle it. Understand that two reasonable people can see the same situation from two completely different viewpoints.

The reason for this is because we are all products of our environment, education, training, and experiences. As an example, experienced and well-trained officers may make a felony stop of a stolen car, using their loudspeaker, strong commands, and with guns drawn. When the occupants of the stolen vehicle turn out to be 13 and 14 years of age, some people may say the conduct of the police officers was unnecessary because "any police officer should be able to handle a 13-year-old child, without the use of their guns."

Perception—that's really the issue in this case, as it is in most controversial cases.

Face the Controversy

Excellent commanders do not shy away from controversy. When confronted with a controversial situation and/or adverse media coverage, they face it head-on. They do not approach it as a win-or-lose situation. They simply face the issues involved in the controversy.

Good commanders recognize that their officers have a difficult and demanding job to do in policing the sometimes "mean streets" of America. The police are routinely called upon to stop people from doing what they want to do, or to force them to do what they don't want to do. This holds true in enforcing every aspect of the law.

That makes the police the coercive arm of government. Police commanders need to understand that police work, by its nature, can put them in direct conflict with lawbreakers, special interest groups and the opinions of individual citizens.

Do Your Homework

While a controversy is still brewing, experienced commanders can read the storm clouds on the horizon. That's the time to start asking questions of your people and gathering information.

Be forceful. If warranted, launch an internal affairs investigation. Interview both commanders and line personnel. Gather incident reports and other facts and figures.

There may be times when your expected controversy never arrives. Don't worry about those rare circumstances because when a real controversy does arrive, your preparation will prove to be a huge asset for you and your department to successfully handle a controversial situation when it does arrive.

Tell the Truth

Unless the police conduct is so egregious as to shock the conscience, most controversial law enforcement situations can be settled with facts, time, and reason. Once the emotions of a situation are calmed by investigation, facts, and leadership, the most reasonable heads will prevail. In time, the issues fade or problems are corrected.

However, when the department remains silent on an issue, or an actual cover-up is detected, the public and the media will keep the controversy alive until heads roll. Historically, the public will not tolerate a government cover-up or lies. So be sure that you have the facts and tell the truth to the public and media. Both will accept reasonable error, but they won't accept cover-ups or lies.

Choose Your Battles

For any commander this issue is critical. All of the foregoing advice can help you make sound decisions on this "fight or flight" segment of handling a controversy. Investigating and doing your homework are steps in the right direction, but there may be other elements to consider in the controversy before making a final stand.

You must examine your department's actions, policies, and procedures in light of current personnel laws and recent court decisions. Commanders must know and understand the federal and state ends of the issue.

However, another set of issues involve the local aspects of any controversial situation. In general, law enforcement is a localized subject. Policing in Plano, Texas is different from policing in Los Angeles, New York, or Chicago. The laws may be similar, but their applications and priorities may be very different. When handling a controversial situation, take local priorities, issues, and customs into consideration.

And—as always—choose your battles well!

Section 6 — Handling Conflict

Yes, conflict is different from controversy, but the process for handling each is very similar.

Human nature being what it is, conflict in the workplace is inevitable. However, your response to those conflicts can determine the success or failure of your operation and possibly the success or failure of your career.

Conflict can arise anywhere in your organization. It may consist of long-term jealousies between two officers. A sergeant in charge of patrol operations may have a major disagreement with a sergeant in charge of covert operations over authority. It can even be a simple case of a personality conflict between two civilians who must still work together on joint projects, but who both work directly for you.

Part of your job as a manager is to be alert for the presence of conflict among all of your people. Minor and temporary disagreements between people may not require immediate action on your part. However, when minor conflicts escalate, and they threaten to disrupt operations, it's time for you to step in and take some action.

Once you recognize that a problem exists, it's time to take action and meet the conflict head-on. However, even after you decide to take action, the way you approach and handle the situation is critical to your success or failure.

To assist you, here are a few hints for handling a conflict situation.

Decide What You Want to Accomplish

Be realistic in setting this goal. You probably can't force people to like each other. On the other hand, you can insist that they work in harmony toward a specific work objective.

As an example, if the chief of investigations and the chief of administration have had a running feud for years, they probably won't become best friends, even at your request. However, you can insist that they make arrangements to cooperate on a study to examine the effectiveness of the current investigations and follow up system. You can also set timetables and set out specific assignments for each.

Once you decide what you want to accomplish, write down your objective and keep it handy. Then you can move on to the next step.

Investigate the Problem

Try to identify the source of the conflict. One of the best ways to do this is to casually discuss the situation with each party involved, individually. Find out how they perceive the situation. As with any investigation, make inquiries of other people who may know something about the situation to get the whole picture. Naturally, keep your inquiries as low key as possible, and keep the responses as confidential as possible.

You may find that the parties involved are unaware that a problem exists. On the other hand, their reaction may indicate a bitter, long-term dislike between two people. Then again, there could simply be a single misunderstanding that has led to the conflict. When your investigation is complete, move on to the next phase.

Call Together the People Who Can Best Settle the Issue

Through your investigation, you should have identified the source of the problem. From that, you probably can identify the people who are involved, and those who can help settle the conflict.

If it was a simple personality conflict between two officers, those two may be all that you need to resolve the issue. In the case of the conflict between the patrol sergeant and the covert operations sergeant over authority, you may need their lieutenant, the personnel officer, or others to help settle the conflict.

Be Ready to Bargain

People will be much more open to reason if they feel that there is some room for negotiation in resolving the situation. If your people feel that the session will merely be a "trip to the woodshed," which will result in downward mandates and threats, they will not be willing to permanently resolve the conflict. However, if they feel there is room for negotiation and that you are open to a fair and just settlement, they will be much more willing to solve the problem on a permanent basis.

Keep Your Objective

Too often during an attempt to settle conflicts, the participants get sidetracked by other issues. During negotiations, refer to the objective you wrote down earlier when you decided what you wanted accomplished. Be sure the conversation and negotiations continue toward that objective.

Avoid the Traps

- Don't focus on the personalities involved, only on their performance.
- Don't get emotionally involved, even though the participants may be.
- Don't choose sides. Merely get to the root of the problem and negotiate a settlement.

Focus on Mutually Beneficial Outcomes

Everyone wants to come out of the meeting a winner. Therefore, direct the meeting so that everyone gains something, even if they have to give up something. If everyone leaves feeling that the conflict was resolved in their favor, then you have done an excellent job.

Ensure That Everyone Understands

Most conflict situations will be resolved by promises of future actions or behavior modifications. Summarize what each individual has agreed to do in the future. Be sure that they understand their role and their specific assignments. Follow up with each individual to ensure there is no misunderstanding about their agreement and assignments.

Follow Up

Ensure that each person involved in the conflict resolution process lives up to his or her end of the agreement. If they don't, then the whole agreement can be jeopardized and the conflict will flare up again. It may even be a worse situation than the first time it occurred.

It will probably be harder to resolve the same conflict the second time around. That's because your credibility, and the credibility of the other parties involved, has been damaged by the inaction and lack of follow-up from the first agreement. Therefore, be sure everyone does it right the first time.

Recognizing conflict as a natural part of people working together can help you to put such problems in their proper perspective. You must also understand that, as a supervisor and manager, it is your duty to minimize and resolve conflict.

Once identified, the proper handling of conflict situations in a calm, orderly, and professional manner, can ensure that your career remains intact and on the road to long-term success.

Section 7 — Forbidden Phrases

There are certain phrases that a modern law enforcement supervisor, at any level, should probably never utter during their business day. Yet, you have heard them all during your career.

The emphasis for a modern-day commander should be on team-building, customer-service, problem-solving, and with a generally positive attitude toward law enforcement resolution.

So, if you hear yourself uttering any of the following phrases, take a reality check for the twenty-first century.

"We Can't Do That"

Whenever you hear that phrase, you should say to yourself, "Why not?"

Modern-day commanders should be open to new ideas, new procedures, and the innovative thinking of the people in their command. It may turn out that a new idea doesn't work out, but at least realistically consider it before rejecting it.

"That's the Way We've Always Done It"

Analogous to #1 above, this phrase is often uttered by the "dinosaur class" of managers.

Law enforcement, as a social service, is always changing to meet the needs of the society that it serves. So change is inevitable and that includes the goals and objectives of the department, as well as certain policies and procedures under which you operate.

Be open to your ever-changing environment.

"You'll Have To …"

Whether you are dealing with a subordinate, a civilian, or a criminal, in today's world you will immediately turn them off with that phrase. The only thing they "have to do" is die and pay taxes. The rest is optional.

Try to relate to them in softer terms such as, "We can solve this problem if we do . . ." or some other, similar phrase. It will work much better with today's public, as well as with your officers.

"Let Me Get Back to You on That"

Whenever you hear this phrase, be wary. You most likely are dealing with somebody who either doesn't want to, or is incapable of, making a decision. You are not likely to ever hear from them again, unless you follow up and press the issue.

Even if you do, their response is likely to be some modified form of, "Let me get back to you on that."

"NO!"

There are times when you just can't accommodate someone's request, but the phrase "NO!", without some explanation or effort to resolve the problem, is generally unacceptable.

Supervisors are generally in a position to make things happen and to make exceptions to general rules. They should be "enablers" not "naysayers."

So, if you must turn down the request of citizens, subordinates, peers, or supervisors, do it diplomatically after exploring any possible alternatives.

"I Don't Know"

Well, maybe you really don't know the answer at this point in time. But that just means that you have to do research until you do know the answer to a customer's or employee's question.

Therefore, you should always add to "I don't know…but I'll do my best to find out and get back to you as soon as possible."

Regardless of whether the question is about a payroll issue from a subordinate, or a legal question from a citizen, you need to find the answer for them.

Yes, you are busy, but the more questions you research early in your career, the more answers you will have later in your career.

These "forbidden phrases" are only a symptom of a greater problem. The problem with people who use such phrases is that they have an attitude problem. Only managers with a negative attitude use these kinds of phrases.

Modern-day supervisors who have a progressive, "can-do" attitude, will never use these phrases. Instead, they use phrases such as, "We can look at that"; We'll work it out"; and "I'll have the answer for you within 48 hours."

So if you ever hear yourself utter any of the negative phrases listed, it's time for an attitude check.

Chapter 5
Earning Respect

If you want to be respected, you must respect yourself.
— Spanish proverb

Section 1 — The Basics of Earning Respect

Section 2 — Are You Fostering Good Morale

Section 3 — Sharing With Your People

Section 4 — Surround Yourself With Competence

Section 5 — Working With Other Agencies

Section 6 — Scoring With Your Bosses

Section 7 — Managing Your Reputation

Section 1 — The Basics of Earning Respect

With every new promotion the department gives you, the insignia and the pay increase. But neither of these give you the respect of the people under your command, nor the respect of your peers or supervisors.

Earning that respect can be difficult for some commanders. You are the newcomer to the unit and all eyes are on you. Everyone attached to the unit will analyze and critique your ability to make decisions, handle personnel, and deal with tough situations. By following a few simple guidelines, you can gain that needed respect.

Set the Standard

Because all eyes are on you, this is your opportunity to show who you are and the ethical and moral standards that you follow. Both on and off duty, be sure to maintain high standards, which will send a clear message as to the standards that you expect from others. They will follow your lead, both consciously and subconsciously.

Always Keep Your Word

Honesty is the greatest attribute that subordinates want in a commander. Always tell the truth and be sure to keep any promises that you make. It is better to under promise and over deliver than break a promise. Your word is your bond—respect and preserve it.

Be Fair

You will be working with a variety of personalities and experience levels. With such diversity in your ranks, it is critical that you treat everyone fairly. Do not play favorites, and always enforce the rules evenhandedly. In doing so, you will not only gain respect, but you will also protect yourself against allegations of actual or perceived discrimination or favoritism. If you engage in favoritism or play political games, you will undermine your own authority, thereby jeopardizing your respect among your coworkers.

Take Care of Your People

Your officers are your most valuable asset. Without them and their support and respect, you cannot be an effective commander. Therefore, whenever possible, you should try to meet their needs. Arrange for the special days off that they need, the special assignment that they want, or that training program they wish to attend. You also need to protect

them from poor assignments, unreasonable expectations, and unfair discipline. Support your people when they need you, and your people will support you when you need them.

Be Humble

Yes, under your command, your unit will thrive and the accolades may flow your way. But when they do, point to your people and say: "They did it." Praise your people, both individually and as a group. Recognize their contributions to the group's achievements. There is no need for you to mention your role in the group's success. These who count will know what your role was. Leadership is about "pointing the way," not taking credit.

Maintain Control

In the often stressed-filled role of a law enforcement commander, you will repeatedly be tested by both street situations and police personnel. How you handle those situations will determine whether you deserve the respect of those involved. Be sure to maintain control of yourself at all times, even when control if the situation may not be clearly defined. How you handle the crisis may be more important than the actual outcome.

During critical situations, others are looking to you for guidance, command presence, and leadership. You must be perceived as a decisive part of the solution if you are to gain the respect of all those who are involved. Your future may depend upon your performance under pressure in any given situation.

Respect is a difficult term to define, but an easy one to spot. Take a look around the room at your next roll call or unit meeting and see how many of your peers and subordinates have your respect. Analyze why and follow your own conclusions. Chances are it is because they earned it.

In your own daily activities, be sure that you are setting the example and leading the way for all with whom you associate. In doing so, you will gain the respect of all those you have contact with. And, you will earn the respect that will ultimately make you a success as an effective commander.

Section 2 — Are You Fostering Good Morale?

Many supervisors don't realize that they are the single greatest influence on the morale of their subordinates. The tone that a supervisor sets, coupled with the quality of their daily decisions and actions, has a greater influence on morale than pay, benefits, or any other single working condition.

You can tell when morale is good in your unit by the positive attitudes of your people, their willingness to cooperate with each other, and their sincere desire to do the best they can at any assignment. However, a good supervisor must constantly nurture and protect good morale to be sure it stays at a high level.

Here are a few tips to help you foster and maintain good morale in your unit.

Maintain a Positive Attitude

You must work at maintaining a good attitude toward your organization, its leadership, and the goals and performance of your unit. Enthusiasm is contagious and your positive attitude will spread to your subordinates.

When everyone has a positive view of their working world, it is easier to complete routine tasks. Problems are minimized and quickly solved through cooperative efforts. Not only is that cooperation good for morale, but it also makes your job as a supervisor easier.

Control Rumors

Negative rumors can quickly destroy good morale in any unit, especially in a law enforcement organization, and especially when left unchecked. Therefore, it is up to the supervisor to take immediate action to control the spread of such rumors. Because most negative rumors are simply distortions of the truth, solid facts are the antidote to be administered by the smart supervisor.

At the first sign of a problem, take the initiative and get the true facts and details—then convey the information to your people. Once the truth comes out, stated by a dependable and credible supervisor, the rumor will be quickly defused and potential problems will disappear. Your immediate action will have helped protect both your people's performance and their morale.

Be Fair to Everyone

Your people watch, talk about, and pass their own judgment on every major action you take as a supervisor. They expect you to exhibit wisdom and fundamental fairness every time you deal with anyone in your command.

If you meet their expectations repeatedly, they will learn to trust you and will feel more secure in their positions. That security can contribute substantially to good morale. Therefore, whenever you are about to make any personnel decision, quietly ask yourself, "Is this action fair to everyone?" "Will it be perceived that way?" If the answer is "Yes" to both, then it's probably a good decision for everyone involved, including you.

Reinforce the Positive

People who feel good about themselves and what they do tend to maintain their own positive attitude and high morale. A supervisor can help foster this natural tendency through a routine of positive reinforcement.

When your people perform well, or apply an innovative solution to a difficult problem, or even just do their job in an excellent manner, let them know that their efforts are noticed and appreciated. Being able to give out such positive reinforcement is one of the benefits of being a supervisor, while at the same time it fosters good attitude and high morale among your subordinates. Both you and your subordinates will feel better about yourselves.

With these few simple, yet sound, supervisory practices, a good supervisor can have a dramatic impact on morale in the unit. Striving to build good morale, then constantly making the effort to protect and maintain it, is a responsibility that any good supervisor needs to understand and implement for the overall success of the unit.

Section 3 — Sharing With Your People

Learning to share things with others was one of the first things you learned in school, if not before. Yet, as a law enforcement leader, that basic concept probably hasn't crossed your mind in years.

What does sharing have to do with your law enforcement career? Try sharing the following items with your subordinates. It may make everyone's job easier.

Sharing Goals

What is the goal of your unit? If you can truly articulate it, then share it with your people. They may not be entirely sure of what the goal of the unit is, or even whether or not it has one. Sorry, "To protect and serve" isn't enough. The goal of your unit must be much more specific, measurable, and attainable. "Reducing robbery by 10% this year" is a goal.

You need to articulate the goals of your unit, then share them with your people. Let them share in the development and defining of the unit's goals and they will be much more willing to share the responsibility for attaining those goals that they will then partially own.

Sharing Your Departmental Culture

Take a quick look at the police departments in your area. Some appear sharp, have good reputations, and seldom have any serious internal problems. Then there are those departments that are known for their poor attitudes, their sloppy appearance, and their internal problems from corruption to brutality.

A police department's culture reflects the values and attitudes of its members in dealing with each other, its civilian employees, and the public. What is the dominant culture of your department? Is it professional and courteous, with integrity beyond reproach? If it is, then share that with your employees. Let them know the kind of professional department they are a part of and that you will stand by them as long as they continue to uphold the level of professional integrity that is expected.

Share Information

As a supervisor you will be among the first to learn of impending promotions, changes in assignments, and a host of other information about the department and its operations. Granted, some of that information should rightfully be kept confidential, but much of it is, or soon will be, common knowledge.

If it is information that will affect your unit, then share it with your people. When the information comes from you, at least they will be sure that they are getting the correct information, untainted by the "rumor mill," which is so active in many departments. Through this sharing of factual information, you will build a mutual trust over time. Then, even when they get a scoop from the rumor mill, they will be more likely to come to you and say, "Hey, is this true?" That's when you'll know you are a successful leader.

Share Learning

If the sharing of day-to-day information is important, so is the sharing of learning. "Knowledge is power," reads an old adage. When you share what you know, or have recently learned, you are sharing your power with your subordinates. Conversely, your people have knowledge that they can share with you and their peers. All that is needed for this sharing to occur is the opportunity and atmosphere to do so.

Set time aside for an exchange of learning in your unit. Take time to talk with each other, but more important, to listen to each other. Whether it's a new interrogation method one of your investigators learned at a recent seminar, or criminal intelligence you picked up from another department, the information needs to be shared within your unit. Make it happen.

Share the Work

Everyone must do their job to make the department work. The chief must get the resources from the politicians to run the department. The highest ranking officers must administer those resources effectively to keep the department running all year. The lieutenants must oversee a variety of units and put out any operational "fires" that crop up. The sergeants make sure the day-to-day things get done, and the officers do their jobs to fulfill their law enforcement duties.

Effective law enforcement is a team effort. Be sure you share the effort of running the team with all of the other members, and make sure that they perform their share of the work for the success of the department.

Caution

Despite the value of sharing things you learned in school and in this article, there are a few things that a successful police commander should *not* share with subordinates. These can include:

- Strictly confidential conversations
- "Need to know only" information
- Certain personnel information, including medical records
- Rumors

And, of course, no police commander should ever share failure. If your unit fails to meet its clearly defined goals, it's solely your responsibility. After all, you were the one in charge.

Section 4 — Surround Yourself With Competence

"Yes men" may be good for your ego, but when it comes to effectively running your organization, you need competence, not compliments.

Because you can't be everywhere all the time, you need trusted subordinates with the background, training, and loyalty to do the right thing, at the right time, for the good of the organization and its goals. You can control your own destiny by consciously developing qualified subordinates so they can eventually take over the running of critical segments of your organization. Once developed properly, those competent individuals are the people who will make you shine.

There are really only five steps in the process of developing subordinates who will be capable of assuming such critical roles, and here they are:

1. ***Identify Winners*** – With an open mind, it's really quite easy to identify those individuals in your organization who have the potential to be successful in the long term. They possess many of the same characteristics you have.

   They generally have a high level of energy. They have enthusiasm for, and a dedication to, the ideals of law enforcement work. They have a solid moral fiber and above-average intelligence. In short, they have the basic skills to be successful in any field, but you are fortunate enough to have them in your command.

2. ***Train Them*** – Even the best people cannot reach their full potential until they are given the tools of their trade and given direction in how to use them. In law enforcement work that means training and education.

   Knowledge is power, and your subordinates need to receive all of the knowledge you can give them if they are to effectively serve your organization. Send them to schools and seminars and direct them to the training resources that will help them in their job now and in the future.

3. ***Groom Them*** – There is much about law enforcement work that is not found in college or academy classrooms. Without that informal knowledge, imparted to them by those who know the ropes, total success can be a difficult battle.

But, just as someone "took you under their wing" many years ago and showed you the way to success, now it is your turn to lead the way for others. Sharing the subtleties of the job with your subordinates, putting them in critical positions, and allowing them to succeed are what mentoring is all about. Let them grow under your direction and guidance, and you will have a loyal and competent coworker for life.

4. ***Encourage Them*** — In many departments, promotions can be few and far between. It is your duty to keep your subordinates motivated during the time they are awaiting an opening for a promotion, so they will be prepared when the opening does occur.

Your praise for their performance in their present position, when warranted, is a powerful motivational tool. Recognition of their efforts to continually improve their abilities through training and education can mean a great deal to them. And, of course, you should encourage them to continue their development for their own benefit as well as for the benefit of the organization.

Be sincere in your praise and encouragement. Your encouragement should stop short of a promise of promotion, but it should provide hope for their future with your department.

5. ***Promote Them*** — When openings do occur, look to your best and most qualified people first. It may be difficult to see over the crafty politician or the smiling approval of the "yes men" or "yes women," but your future success depends on placing the most competent people in your most critical positions.

In most cases, you are the boss and can choose who you want in those positions. You want your own team players, and, if you have done your job, they are waiting at the sidelines, eager and ready to get into the game, and to make you a winner.

Section 5 — Working With Other Agencies

Despite its importance, your unit is probably only one of many government and non-government agencies that serve your ultimate objective. When it is necessary for your unit to work with, through, or around another agency, conflicts and problems can develop. When they do, the fallout can race up the chain of command and land directly in your lap, sometimes with little or no warning.

Whether it involves logistical, operational, or political problems, your management skills will be tested. The actions that you take can either fuel the situation and send it to a higher level, or defuse it. Coming to an equitable solution that satisfies all of the agencies and gets the job done should be your goal.

The following simple guidelines can help you minimize the problems and maximize the results of your interagency efforts.

Understand Their Perspective

Before interacting with another agency, take time to consider the other agency's position and look at the differences between how they operate and how your unit operates. Your unit may work around the clock, seven days a week; theirs may work only regular business hours. You may have an overtime budget or not be required to pay overtime. Many agencies in both the public and private sector have no overtime budgets. Your agency may be military or paramilitary; theirs may be strictly civilian. You may have strict procedural guidelines; theirs may have very loose guidelines.

Each agency operates according to its own unique policies, priorities, and schedules, and their missions and goals are likely to be very different from yours. In addition, few agencies share the sense of urgency that comes with working as a protection or public safety agency. Your request may be honored, but the other agency's may have to be rescheduled, and it will be done only on their normal workdays.

These kinds of differences can ultimately be worked out between professionals in each of the respective agencies. But understanding each other's situations can help smooth the path to a solution and eliminate some initial frustrations for both agencies.

Sell! — Don't Tell

Special unit commanders know what they want and when they want it. They can generally issue an order and it gets carried out quickly in their military or paramilitary environment. Taking that same approach in dealing with a civilian agency will probably get you nowhere.

When requesting a service, or cooperation from another agency, be prepared to have to sell the other agency's decision-makers on what you need, why you need it, and why they should assist you. Be prepared to state your case in detail, often to more than one person, until you can sell the right person to give the decision the go-ahead.

Being demanding or officious will probably not get the results you want, because the members of the other agency don't work for you. However, selling your request professionally may get them to work with you.

Stay calm and be reasonable.

Chances are that before the situation or problem ever got to you, someone else had tried unsuccessfully to get the job done. In doing so, he or she may have muddied the waters and turned the whole situation into a power struggle or an emotionally charged issue.

Try to make your own entry into the situation as calm and rational as possible. Avoid getting caught up in the emotional firestorm that may have forced it to your level in the first place. Take your time and carefully gather the facts that can separate the issues from the emotions. Focus on what is really needed to defuse the situation so that both agencies can move forward.

Once you have focused on the problem, negotiate a fair and equitable solution. Once you have gotten what you want, get out. Don't push unreasonably for additional concessions.

Always try to leave on good terms, because you will probably have to deal with that agency again in the future. A great ending is something like "Call me personally if a situation like this ever develops again and you and I will work it out together."

Who Should Do It?

Interagency conflicts should be worked out at the lowest possible level in the organization, consistent with existing policies. If an individual has the power to solve the problem, then they should do so. Kicking it up to a higher authority for resolution generally indicates a lack of initiative or poor management-level skills. It also escalates the situation and generally delays the decision and its implementation.

Resolve conflicts with your peer in the other agency. "Peer" means someone of an equivalent rank or position who has about the same authority in their organization as you do in your organization. Be sure that both of you have the power and authority to implement any agreement you reach.

If, after using all of your negotiation and management skills, you still cannot resolve the conflict, then it is appropriate for you to go to your boss with the problem. Your boss should then either resolve it at his/her level or clear the way for it to come back to you for final resolution.

Minor, and sometimes major, interagency problems and conflicts are an everyday part of the workings of both governmental and private agencies in any operation. Accept their existence and work with each one as necessary. Handling them effectively is a part of making operations successful, which is the biggest part of your job as an operations manager.

Section 6 — Scoring With Your Bosses

Whether your boss is the city manager, a tough lieutenant, or the chief of police, you need to know how to work with them for their benefit, the benefit of your department, and for your future job security. If you have the ability to make their life easier, rest assured that they will instinctively make your life easier.

Keep in mind that policing is a people-to-people business. The people involved are many and varied. There is the public—on both sides of the law. There are politicians and commanders of all ranks, and all need to know how you can help them. It may sound difficult, but as a professional police commander, you may find it quite easy to satisfy these competing interests if you are willing to follow these few simple guidelines:

- ***Do Your Best*** — You are not perfect. Yet you need to constantly try to do the right thing at the right time. You need to make timely and competent decisions at the time and place that they need to be made. Then, stand by those decisions. By doing so, you will gain the respect of those you work with, including your bosses, your peers, and your "people."

- ***Take Ownership*** — Whether your domain is a shift, a precinct, or an entire community, it is your responsibility to police it effectively. That means different things to different communities. In some, it is your responsibility as a police commander to "keep the lid on," and that's it. In other communities, your goal is to maintain security and a perception of safety for your citizens. Whatever your community wants of you, you and your people should deliver what they want from their police department.

- ***Deliver More Than You Promise*** – There are minimal standards that your boss and the community will require from you as a police commander. Do more!

  A police leader will spend the time and effort to not only get the job of basic policing done, but will spend the extra time and effort to ensure excellence in every aspect of the policing effort.

- ***Have a Passion for Your Job*** – If you get excited about coming to work and doing your job as a police supervisor that enthusiasm will serve as an example to your people. Be upbeat and enthusiastic about enforcing the law, guarding constitutional rights, and serving the public, and your people will also be enthusiastic about doing the same.

- ***Be Customer Driven*** – Whether you are working with a city manager, a fellow supervisor, or the complainant of a minor crime, keep in mind who they are, their concerns, and your position and influence on their current plight. Professional police work involves empathy, understanding, and appropriate action on your part. Make it all happen.

- ***Meet the Challenges*** – In the new millennium, policing poses challenges unknown to previous generations of police supervisors. Meeting those challenges requires a new breed of professional, educated, and astute police supervisors. Managing a new and diverse generation of police officers offers even more challenges than our predecessors faced.

  Recognizing the challenges and changes is a milestone for police supervisors. Meeting those challenges and changes is the task before you. Do well and you will succeed; fail and you will face unemployment.

- ***Develop Your People Skills*** – In order to be a successful police commander, you will be required to have good people skills. You must have the ability to command without appearing officious. You must be able to develop the confidence and loyalty of the people both above and below you in your organization. This does not "just happen." You must develop a relationship with your people, over time, through the strength of your personality, and by exhibiting your skills and abilities in your everyday actions.

So what does all of this have to do with "Scoring with Your Bosses?"

Rest assured that they are always watching. They are in contact with your subordinates and your peers. They know your reputation as either a firm, solid commander who they can trust to get the job done—or as something else.

Try to "score with your bosses" by working hard at every aspect of your job. Treat everyone fairly and always try to do "the right thing." In doing so, you will automatically score with your bosses and not even know it.

Next thing you know, you will be promoted again.

Section 7 — Managing Your Reputation

Who are you? You may have one opinion, while your bosses, peers, and subordinates have completely different opinions about you and your performance as a law enforcement supervisor.

Are these different opinions legitimate? Should they be of concern to you? Who controls your personal reputation? Who controls your professional reputation?

Here are some guidelines so that you are in control of your reputation and, subsequently, your effectiveness as a supervisor.

Your Personal Reputation

Are you honest or dishonest? Are you a person of your word, backed up by your actions or are you a wishy-washy opportunist? Is your integrity your watchword or is: "What's in it for me?" the phrase you live by?

Regardless of what your answers are, you will be judged by everything in your public and private life. These individuals will judge you by the moral standards you live by.

Those standards establish both your personal reputation and your professional reputation.

A Commanding Reputation

Do you take command? Or have you been given a position that you cannot fulfill as commander? Leadership is action, not position. To be considered an effective commander, you must have the training, education, and experience to effectively fill your position.

In addition, you must know and understand the mission of your department and must support its objectives. You must be loyal and dedicated to the goals of the department, subordinate officers, and to the community that you serve. And, you must make the correct decisions worthy of someone who calls himself or herself a commander.

Your Reputation With Your Unit

The people in your unit are in the best position to observe your day-to-day activities and therefore to legitimately enhance or detract from your overall reputation. They closely observe your everyday actions, attitudes, and decisions.

If you are fair, they observe you as fair. If you are knowledgeable, they observe you as knowledgeable. If you are decisive, they observe you as decisive.

You cannot hide from them. They observe, judge, and form their own opinions about you as a boss and a leader. And they will spread the word about their opinions—one way or the other!

Your Reputation as a Member of the Department

How do you represent your department? Do you look like a professional officer? Are your shoes shined, your hair cut, and your pants pressed? Do you have a positive, "How can I help you?" attitude toward the public? Or do you have an arrogant, self-serving, "us versus them" attitude? Your people, both higher and lower in rank, will evaluate you on this. They will be your "departmental judge," while the public will be the external judge of your appearance, attitude, and demeanor.

Your Professional Reputation

Law enforcement continually seeks recognition as a profession similar to doctors, lawyers, accountants, and teachers. Does your reputation warrant recognition as representative of such a profession?

Do you have a four-year college degree in your profession? Do you adhere to the professional standards set out by law enforcement's most professional organizations? Do you exemplify the image of a professional law enforcement officer and commander in every way—from your personal life to the professional standards of the law enforcement profession? Do you adhere to the Law Enforcement Code of Ethics in all of your daily activities?

Your reputation as a professional law enforcement officer is critical to your success. As a police officer, your reputation as a fair and just officer—even among the criminal element—can determine whether you quietly execute a routine arrest or whether it ends up in controversy. Now, as you seek to climb the ladder of success to progressively higher ranks, your success also depends largely on your reputation. This is particularly true in larger departments where you may not be personally known, but may be well known by your reputation as an effective or ineffective commander.

If you want to be upwardly mobile, in your department, you need to seriously work on obtaining and maintaining an impeccable reputation, both personally and professionally. To enhance your reputation in any organization, always try to do the right thing, whether that is getting the best education or training that you can, or by simply treating a subordinate or "perp" the right way. If you do, you will continually exhibit professionalism—and that is what good reputations are made of!

Chapter 6
Fostering Loyalty

When you are part of a team, you stand up for your teammates. Your loyalty is to them. You protect them through good and bad because they'd do the same for you.

— Yogi Berra

Section 1 — The Definition of Loyalty

Section 2 — Loyalty — You Can't Succeed Without It

Section 3 — Identifying the Winners in Your Department

Section 4 — Helping New Supervisors Succeed

Section 5 — Training the Newly Promoted Supervisor

Section 6 — Working With Other Commanders

Section 7 — Developing Future Leaders

Section 1 — The Definition of Loyalty

Loyalty is one of those terms that defies a clear-cut definition. Yet we all know loyalty when we see it—or do we?

Commanders don't often think about loyalty until they start looking for it. This usually occurs during an operational or administrative crisis, when the commander needs the physical, moral, or emotional support of their subordinates. For good commanders, loyalty is there when it is needed. For poor commanders, it is not.

To ensure that loyalty of subordinates is there when needed, commanders need to plan ahead. Loyalty must be developed over time, and it has many facets.

The legendary General George S. Patton recognized the responsibilities of a commander in developing loyalty among his subordinates. In his book, *War As I Knew It*, he stated, "There is a great deal of talk about loyalty from the bottom to the top. Loyalty from the top down is even more necessary and much less prevalent."

To develop a sense of loyalty among his subordinates, a commander must develop a positive rapport with them. The commander must get to know his people personally. Yes, they are workers, but they are first and foremost, people. Each of them is unique and needs to be treated accordingly.

A commander must also help them do their jobs more easily by clearing out red tape and other stumbling blocks.. As management expert Peter Drucker said, "So much of what we call management consists of making it difficult for people to do their jobs." A good commander ensures that his people encounter as few bureaucratic impediments as possible.

The commander must also train and develop his people so that they can maximize their individual potential to reach their selected goals. Proper training and development help them to maximize their own potential. It allows them to grow and blossom into future commanders themselves. But without the proper guidance and mentoring, they will not reach their full potential and their careers and enthusiasm will be stunted.

A good commander must also watch out for his people, protecting them from unreasonable and arbitrary decisions that adversely affect them. The commander must reasonably ensure their safety and health on the job as well. In general, he must be a guardian of his people.

These actions will help subordinates learn to trust their commander. Over time, that trust will develop into a loyalty that both the commander and the subordinate can rely on.

However, a commander's responsibility for loyalty does not apply only to dealings with subordinates. A commander also has loyalty responsibilities to his superiors. General Malin Craig made that point clear to a graduating class at West Point when he told them, "An officer … should make it a cardinal principle of life that by no act of commission or omission on his part will he permit his immediate superior to make a mistake."

Just as you, as a commander, want and need the loyalty of your subordinates, so does your boss want and need your loyalty.

There is also a need to develop loyalty among your peers, and for you to be loyal to them. Problems often cross unit and departmental lines. During a crisis, a commander has one less concern when he knows he can rely on his peers to help when they are needed.

And, of course, a good commander is loyal to his or her own ideals and standards of conduct. Good commanders never compromise their honesty, integrity, or commitment to do less than their best in all aspects of their duties.

Loyalty can be defined as a state of mutual respect, admiration, and commitment. You must maintain that type of relationship with those above, below, and parallel to you on the organizational chart. All of them require your loyalty, if you are to expect them to be loyal to you when you need them.

Section 2 — Loyalty — You Can't Succeed Without It

As a law enforcement commander, you need loyal employees who will support you, follow you, and protect you. Whether you are assigned to front-line operations or administration, the loyalty of your subordinates is critical to your success and well-being.

Yet few commanders think about loyalty until they need it. Then they expect that their loyal following will be there to support and protect them. Maybe it will be—maybe it won't be.

Smart commanders develop loyalty among their subordinates long before they need it. They recognize that loyalty is a two-way street. To gain the loyalty of your subordinates, you must be loyal to them.

To help you, here are a few tips on developing loyalty.

Be Pleasant and Approachable

Loyalty starts out by having a mutually good feeling about the other person. A smile and a warm "Good morning" are a good starting place. Over time, your pleasant attitude and approachability will help foster an atmosphere of mutual understanding and commitment.

Know Your People

Your people are your most valuable asset as a law enforcement commander. However, they are people, not objects, and should be treated accordingly.

Get to know them as people. Ask about their hobbies and interests. Ask about their families, their health, and their vacations. Take a genuine interest in them.

Learn their strengths and their weaknesses. Steer them in the right direction so they can maximize their own potential to reach their goals.

Help Your People to Do Their Jobs

As commander, you are in a position to eliminate stumbling blocks to the successful completion of your subordinates' tasks. You may have to cut some red tape for them, make sure they have the right equipment, or assign more resources to help them. But most important, be sure that you give them the encouragement they need to perform their most difficult tasks.

Train and Develop Your People

If employees are well trained, they do what is expected of them confidently and willingly. However, a lack of proper training can make their tasks difficult and uncomfortable. As a good commander, ensure that they get the training they need. Tell them what you expect from them. Take time with them until they have learned the job thoroughly and can do the job comfortably.

After that, teach them new or easier ways of doing their jobs. Encourage them to learn new skills, either on or off the job. In fact, arrange for it by making them aware of schools, seminars, training sessions, and new technology. The new skills they learn will help them to grow, and it will lead to your being able to rely on them for new projects or increased responsibilities.

The rapport you build with your employees will result in a closer mutual respect and loyalty.

Watch Out for Your People

As a commander, you must protect your people from unreasonable rules or poor decisions that can adversely affect them. You must recognize their views and perspectives and represent them to your supervisors.

When your subordinates make an error, help minimize the effect of that error. You may also be able to minimize the consequences they face in a disciplinary action.

Good commanders know that they too will make an error some day that a subordinate might be able to help correct. If the commander has watched out for and helped his subordinates in the past, he can expect their help when it is needed.

Loyalty is a difficult term to actually define, yet we all know it when we see it. It cannot be forced on demand. It is developed over time through an ongoing series of events leading to the feelings of mutual trust and admiration that we call loyalty. A commander cannot be successful without it.

Section 3 — Identifying the Winners in Your Department

When you look around your department, it's very easy to identify the "winners." A winner is the captain who had a meteoric rise to his current rank. It could be the detective who consistently cracks big cases. It could even be the patrol officer who seems to just naturally "stumble" over heavy-duty criminals while on patrol.

It's great to have winners on your team in any department or unit. At first glance, these winners just seem to come by their winning ways naturally. But a closer analysis of their traits and habits can reveal a pattern of conduct that *makes* them all winners in their respective areas of expertise.

Here are ten traits of those people you can readily identify as "winners":

1. ***They Maintain a Positive Attitude*** – Winners are optimists. They view the world as their own personal playground. They have a good sense of humor and laugh easily. They always see the positive, not the negative, side of a situation. As a result they are always "up" and projecting a positive attitude toward their work and their co-workers.

2. ***They Solve Problems*** – When obstacles appear in their path, they view them as only a temporary situation. They enjoy the challenge of finding a solution, clearing the obstacle, and moving forward. In general, they work to solve their own problems without having to get their supervisors involved. That makes them appear even more competent to their bosses and peers.

3. ***They Make Decisions*** – Winners are decisive. They quickly gather the facts in a difficult situation, formulate possible solutions, and choose what they believe is the best option. By making such decisions, they get things done. While others are still gathering facts, the winner already has the results from their decision and has taken action.

4. ***They Seek and Enjoy New Experiences*** – The winners enjoy their work because no two days are alike. Winners enjoy the thrill of the unknown. They volunteer for special assignments to expand their horizons and gain new experiences. The resulting broad-based knowledge and experience allows them to bring more to their jobs than the other less adventurous members of their unit. Therefore, their overall performance becomes better.

5. ***They Manage Their Time Effectively*** – When the goal is to arrest criminals, winners go where the criminals are. They focus their activities where they can get the highest rate of return for the time they spend. They recognize that they generally won't find criminals in a locker room, coffee shop, or restaurant. They will find criminals on the street, during traffic stops, and while actively pursuing investigations. As a result, their numbers are higher than other members of their units.

6. ***They Invest in Self-Improvement*** – Although their self-improvement efforts may not be readily visible, winners work hard at being good at their jobs. They get technical knowledge as well as new ideas by reading and attending courses and seminars. As a result, winners are the most knowledgeable and effective members of their unit or specialty area.

7. ***They Are Friendly Toward Others*** – The adage about catching more flies with honey than with vinegar is appropriate here.

Whether dealing with coworkers, citizens, or criminals, winners are appropriately friendly with all. As a result, coworkers like them and readily help them when needed. Citizens are happy with their performance and criminals are more willing to open up to them and provide information or confessions to them.

8. ***They Serve the Needs of Others*** – Winners, at any level, try to help their fellow man or woman. In helping to solve others' problems, they build a rapport, develop a friendship, and show genuine interest in the needs of others. Winners are generally paid back in kind for their efforts on behalf of others.

9. ***They Balance Work, Play, and Rest*** – For all of their intense efforts at work, winners also recognize that work is only one aspect of their life. They balance their success at work with family, friends, and off-duty activities. They are often winners in all of these areas, because they balance their lives appropriately.

10. ***They Control Their Own Destinies*** – Winners are in control of their performance and their lives. They know how to perform their jobs well while avoiding the problems that plague others. Because they are in charge of their lives, they look like they are in charge of their lives. And that's why they are so easy to spot in your department.

Share these ten simple secrets for becoming a winner with your subordinates. Over time, you'll be amazed at how many more winners you will have on your team. Of course, then they will also want to work for the winner in you. Everybody loves a winner!

Section 4 — Helping New Supervisors Succeed

Making the transition from being a line police officer to becoming a police supervisor is the most profound career change an officer will face. Despite that fact the majority of newly promoted police supervisors will not be adequately prepared to take on their new assignments. Worse yet is that their superiors in the department may not realize these new subordinate supervisors need help to succeed in their assignments as police supervisors.

In policing today, there are still some officers who were merely thrust into the job of police officer with little or no formal training. "Common sense is all you need to be a good cop," one police administrator said in an interview. It may be true that common sense is a big part of successful policing, but in today's demanding and highly litigious environment, no rational police chief or sheriff would put an officer on the street without sending him or her to a formal academy for several weeks or months.

Yet when police officers are promoted to the supervisory rank of corporal, sergeant, or lieutenant, it is apparently assumed they will succeed at their new job with limited, or no, training, guidance, or support from the rest of the members of their "management team."

Certainly you want to be sure that your management team is doing everything they can to help your new police supervisors succeed. Here are a few critical areas to check to be sure your department is doing everything for your new supervisor's success.

Promotional Preparation

Do your officers know what they have to do to get promoted?

Professional departments analyze the duties and the criteria that make a good police supervisor. Then they set out minimum standards to be considered for promotion.

A wide variety of standards exist, dependent on the mission of the individual department. However, most professional departments include a minimum number of college credits toward a criminal justice or management degree as a part of the criteria. Many also include the successful completion of a written exam based on the laws of the particular jurisdiction, and the policies and procedures of the department. Yet another component of the promotional process may include knowledge of basic management theories and processes as exhibited through written or oral examinations. And finally, successful completion of an oral board or assessment center to exhibit an understanding of the duties and responsibilities of being a successful police supervisor.

With an adequate promotional preparation program in effect, line officers know how to prepare for a promotion. Administrators will also know that their candidates will possess the basic knowledge and understanding of the role of a police supervisor.

Supervisory Training — *Before* Assuming a Command

Perhaps the gravest error some administrators commit is that they promote new supervisors and thrust them into their new assignments with absolutely no training. Even where states mandate supervisory training for police supervisors the language of the law is often couched in terms such as, "must attend _____ hours of supervisory training within one year of promotion."

Too often this phrase is realistically interpreted as "within one year after promotion." To many busy police administrators, this play on words may seem relatively insignificant.

However, to the newly promoted supervisor, these words are very significant. From their standpoint, they are thrust into a supervisory position with no training or guidance. In essence, they are forced to 'sink or swim' in their new position. They are given up to a year without training to make mistakes, ruin their reputation, or face some degree of supervisory liability without any training.

In today's environment, police administrators wouldn't think about putting a police officer on the street without academy training, yet many administrators put police supervisors on the street with no training.

A Supervisory FTO Program

In a time when we talk very freely about "role models" for our children, we also provide successful field training officers (FTOs) for our new recruits immediately after their basic training. In professional organizations these FTOs are the best police officers the department has. It is left to them to be the role models for our new officers to emulate in the performance of their duties.

Yet many departments fail to recognize the value of successful police supervisors to act as role models for newly promoted supervisors. New supervisors are often expected to succeed based on their observations of the performance of their police corporals, sergeants, and lieutenants. That's fine if their supervisory role models were highly trained professional examples of what a police supervisor should be.

But what if they weren't? Then their negative traits would also be passed on to the new supervisor.

A supervisory FTO program using the best police supervisors can pay great dividends to a department over time.

Backing and Support

A police administrator must be willing to underwrite the honest mistakes of his/her subordinates. This is particularly important in the case of newly appointed police supervisors.

After the formal preparation of reading, schools, and an FTO program, the final evaluation of a supervisor is how they perform on their own in real world situations. Their ability to apply their formal education to real world situations involving people and emotions is the true test of their worth as a supervisor.

However, as we all learned in our own trial-and-error sessions, supervisors are seldom 100% correct or 100% wrong. Virtually all supervisory decisions are somewhat correct given the limitations of the facts known at the time and place that the supervisory decisions needed to be made.

Unless the effect of the new supervisor's decision clearly violates law, rules, or policy, the police administrator should make every effort to provide backing and support to the subordinate supervisor's decision. To do otherwise undermines the new supervisor's judgment and authority. To support their decisions bolsters their authority, credibility, and their faith in their own judgment.

Given the difficulty of the transition from being a line officer to being a front-line supervisor, police administrators need to be particularly sensitive to the needs of the newly promoted. Although you may have toughed it out to make the grade, today's new supervisor faces a much more complex world in policing.

It is incumbent on you to help them succeed in every way you can, which is good for them, for you, and for the future of the department.

Section 5 — Training the Newly Promoted Supervisor

It was a match made in heaven.

When Sergeant Broderick retired after ten years as the midnight-shift commander in a small police department, his replacement was waiting in the wings. Officer John Remy had worked nights under the old Sarge for three years. He was young, but also bright, articulate, dependable, and he looked great in uniform. He got along with everybody. His family situation assured that he would want to work nights for a long time to come.

When Remy was advised that he would be a sergeant, he was elated. He could use the raise in pay, although he did express some reservation about being able to fill Sergeant Broderick's shoes. A little reassurance and he was sure he could handle the job.

All was well—or was it?

The new sergeant's first month was tough. On one occasion, he had not notified his supervisor about an officer who was injured during his shift, nor had he completed a report on the incident. The sergeant's routine reports were late in coming in. There were informal reports of two officers being off-post repeatedly. Several times officers were late reporting for duty on Sgt. Remy's shift. Worse yet, two of the most dependable officers on midnights had suddenly requested transfers to other shifts. There were other problems as well.

What went wrong? How could a promotion that appeared so right go so wrong?

All too often, police administrators with 20-plus years of experience forget how difficult the transition from patrolman to sergeant was for them. In today's working environment, it can be even tougher than it was then.

The workforce is different than it was years ago. Technology has made our lives easier in one way, but the pressures on a police supervisor are greater than ever before. More and better reports are required due to the liability explosion. Even the laws governing employees and the workplace have become more complex and harder to understand, particularly for new supervisors.

Old Sergeant Broderick had eased into these new supervisory and administrative responsibilities. Young Sergeant Remy was thrust into them and subsequently overwhelmed.

The young Sergeant might still survive, but he will have an uphill battle to change the impressions he had given to both his subordinates and the administration. It will take its toll on him in stress and frustration. It will also cost the department a great deal in terms of lost morale, attrition, and increased administrative problems. There may even be a liability cost in terms of problems generated during the new sergeant's transition period.

The sad thing is that many of these problems could have been prevented with proper advance training. But training is expensive and time consuming; true, but so are the problems created by the failure to train. The television ad that espouses the phrase "Pay me now, or pay me later," accurately hits the mark in this case.

In one survey, experienced supervisors were asked to list common mistakes made by new supervisors. The list ranged from "failed to make timely decisions" to "tried to be one of the guys." Other comments included "gave only negative criticism," "showed favoritism," "made serious administrative errors," and "didn't know when to seek advice or notify superiors."

All of these errors, and the majority of others, can be easily prevented through proper training *before* the person assumes their new duties.

The newly appointed supervisor wants to learn to do the job right. Because training programs are available to teach basic supervisory skills at most regional academies, there is little excuse for not getting them the training they so desperately need to succeed in their new position.

On-the-job training can also be an excellent way to ease new supervisors into their positions. The new supervisor gets to learn the actual duties and responsibilities of the position under the guidance of an experienced hand. Of course, he may also pick up some of the bad habits or cynicism of the more experienced supervisor in the process, but a good selection process can solve most of that problem.

The best alternative is to arm the new supervisor with a combination of both of these instructional alternatives. Approved outside classroom training and properly prepared in-house training programs can set out the guidelines for the supervisor and what he or she can expect in the way of support from the department. The new member of the supervisory team should then be given adequate time to work with the best and most experienced person available who holds down the same, or a very similar, position. Ideally, he should work with the supervisor of the men and women he will be supervising so that he can get to know them and they can get to know him.

Whatever program or combination of programs you choose, each segment should be well-defined, properly planned, and adequately executed by competent, experienced instructors.

After adequate classroom and on-the-job training, many of the potential problems will have been prevented. Given proper direction and instruction, the new supervisor will feel better prepared and more secure as he or she assumes his or her new position. The new sergeant's subordinates will be happier and you will sleep better during the midnight shift knowing that a well-trained, prepared, and competent Sergeant Remy is in charge.

Section 6 – Working With Other Commanders

Working in harmony with other officers, department heads, specialized units, and other departments requires a special awareness and expertise from a law enforcement commander. This interaction can be an enjoyable experience for competent managers; or it can be an experience full of career-damaging pitfalls, problems, and lawsuits for the uninitiated police manager.

Your department's policy and procedure manual may cover all, or some, of the following situations. If it does, be sure to follow it. If it doesn't, then here are a few tips to help you work through multiple command, or no command, situations.

Safety First

Although the mission of your unit is important, the safety of your personnel is of paramount importance. Your people must go home safely at the end of the day, and must be available to work to fulfill your overall mission on future days and shifts.

When other units are involved in your operations, be sure to protect the safety of your people. When detectives want to use uniformed members up front on a drug raid, be sure that reasonable safeguards are in place to assure the safety of those uniformed officers. Cooperate with the detectives, but be sure you reach a mutual agreement on the activities and safety of both units in the process.

When the SWAT unit needs an outer perimeter to cover their operations, leave the SWAT activities to their commander, but be sure that your people are adequately protected if the operation spills out to your perimeter. Be sure to brief your people on contingency plans and possibilities. And, be sure that the SWAT commander recognizes and respects the fact that your people do not have the heavy equipment or tactical training of his unit. Let him know that he has a responsibility to your units as well as his own.

Specialized Units

In crowd control or riot situations, you may find yourself working with some specialized units, *ad hoc*, and sometimes reluctantly. At this point of necessity, and the arrival of the specialized unit's troops, you must assume the leadership role, consistent with the policies and procedures of your department's manual and protocol.

The specialized units may include K-9 units, tactical teams, or other specialized personnel. If possible, be sure that you are in close contact with each unit's commander. This can be difficult in a riot or other chaotic situation, so prior planning can be important. You must work with your peer in the other unit to be sure the overall mission is agreed on, and be sure that the means to the end is agreed on. Many times, the individual units are not in agreement on the objective, the force to be used, or the overall mission, so you must be prepared to deal with such a situation.

Internal Strife

Any good commander recognizes that reasonable people can disagree, even in critical situations. However, somebody must assume the leadership role and be in charge. That, by definition, requires someone in the organization to step forward and execute dominion and control over the situation, and often, other units. You are either "in charge," or "following," at this point.

In critical situations, there can be only brief internal strife. You must make the decision to either assume the leadership role, or commit your unit to the mission established by one of your peers who has chosen to assume the leadership role. The decision is up to you, but you cannot hesitate in critical situations. To do so may endanger the mission, as well as the safety of your personnel. Disagreement and indecision are the materials that injuries and lawsuits are made of in police work.

Command Vacuum

Occasionally, a command vacuum is created by the loss or separation of a unit's commander from the main body. This can spell disaster or defeat for a police unit, just as it can for a military unit in critical situations. If there is no commander of appropriate rank available for the specialized unit, and you are of an appropriate rank, then you must take charge and make the appropriate assignments of personnel consistent with the department's overall objective under the circumstances.

Be sure to work with the highest available ranking member of the specialized unit so that you understand the capabilities of their unit and ensure that they understand the department's overall objective in the situation. Do not commit them to any action until you are both in agreement on their objective, and the methods to be used to reach that objective.

If you are the ranking officer in one of these critical situations, be sure to remember the phrase, "When in charge, take charge." It will serve you well.

Consensus

When time is not of the essence, you should reach out to your coworkers who are in charge of other units, precincts, or specialty areas. Develop a personal relationship and professional rapport with them. Get to know them and the capabilities of their units. This informal interaction, in a non-stress situation, will give you the opportunity to learn about other units, their commanders, and capabilities, and will help you to know whom you can and cannot depend on in future critical situations.

You can leave command cooperation to chance, and hope all works out well in a critical situation, or you can take control of it long before it happens. It is all up to you as a competent commander of your unit, who has to rely on and work with a variety of other units and commanders. But the time to think about who will be in charge of whom, and when, should be resolved in your mind now—not when your unit, and others, are taking rocks and bottles in a riot situation.

Section 7 — Developing Future Leaders

You may have been an excellent street officer. But then, you were only responsible for your own actions. The role of sergeant might not have been too bad for you. That's when you directed six to ten other officers. You were responsible for their actions, but you had direct control of them.

However, as you reach the second and third levels of command and above, you quickly recognize that you can't do it all anymore. You are now in charge of, and ultimately responsible for, the actions of tens, hundreds, or even thousands of officers. You need help!

Where will you find the competent assistants you need; those sergeants, lieutenants and captains who keep your police department running as a professional organization? Well, you had better have thought in terms of personnel development long before you assumed your current command, or you and your department could be in big trouble. The lack of good command personnel—leaders—is why many departments develop serious personnel, morale and ethical problems.

To ensure that you have a number of good, solid leaders to draw from as you climb through the ranks, here are a few tips about developing those future leaders for the time when they are needed.

Identify Future Leaders

In reality, this is the easiest part of your personnel development responsibility. You need only recognize leadership potential as it identifies itself to you. You can recognize potential leaders easily. They exhibit many of the same qualities that you possess.

They are intelligent, knowledgeable, professional, and dedicated. They arrive early, stay late, and are always willing to take on a little more responsibility than their peers. It is clear by their actions and attitudes that they are willing to do the right thing at the right time in all circumstances. In fact, they almost have "future leader" stamped on their forehead, if only you can read it.

Become Their Mentor

Once individuals have identified themselves as having leadership potential, that's when your work really begins. To reach their potential, those individuals need someone to provide them with advice and guidance on how to maximize their chances of becoming successful leaders.

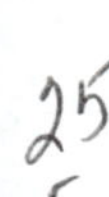

Because you have already "been there," your advice and guidance can be of great value to them. You know and understand the mission and the policies, procedures, and politics of your particular department. You also know what it takes to be a successful commander. You now need to share that, over time, with those persons who have leadership potential. Being an excellent role model is good, but mentoring requires more overt actions on your part.

Make a Plan

You wouldn't embark on a long journey without some kind of a plan in place to help you with directions and resources along the way. Nor would you try to build a building without a blueprint or some other solid building plan in place. Therefore it follows that to build a career that will span 20 to 30 years also requires a solid plan to reach its final goal.

In police work, education, training, and experience are the building blocks for a successful career. It is up to you to help your future commanders build the knowledge and skills they will need to meet the challenges of the future. Work with them and encourage them. Help them put a plan in place that will help them become the successful law enforcement leaders of the future in your department.

Monitor Their Careers

As your people work their way up through the ranks, they will be tested many times. They will have triumphs and setbacks. It is up to you to help them through the ups and downs of their career path. You can help them to be neither elated over their victories nor crushed by their defeats. In short, you can help them to mature.

Keep in touch with them. Be sure you send a note of congratulations to them on their promotions or a note of encouragement as they face adversity. In addition to the face value of your notes, you will also be developing their loyalty to you as their mentor, even if you are not currently in their direct chain of command.

Enjoy the Trip

Among all of the rewards of being a commander, one of the greatest is watching a protégé climb the ranks toward a successful career. Watching that spark of leadership potential you saw in a young recruit build in intensity into a successful command officer is among the greatest feelings you will experience as a command officer.

That alone might make the effort worthwhile, but there are other rewards for your efforts of developing your people. One is that as you progress up your own career ladder, you will have competent personnel, whom you know and trust, to place in key positions to help you accomplish your current mission.

But the final reward is that when you finally move on to your retirement years, you will have a trusted colleague to replace you. And that will leave you with the satisfying feeling that your department and your community are in solid and competent hands—thanks to your efforts.

Chapter 7
Administrative Survival

We can lick gravity, but sometimes the paperwork is overwhelming.
— Werner von Braun

Section 1 — Administrative Survival

Section 2 — Getting a Handle on Your Time

Section 3 — Managing that Endless Line of Meetings

Section 4 — Handling Information Overload

Section 5 — Delegate — But Do It Right!

Section 6 — Career Traps

Section 1 — Administrative Survival

Many excellent police officers get promoted only to fall flat on their faces as supervisors.

They have no trouble with their duties as a supervisor. Their new-found problems are in the unfamiliar arena of administration. They are plagued by missed deadlines, lost reports, an unfamiliar bureaucracy, and a lack of time to make it all better.

Here are some survival tips to help you, or your new supervisor, navigate through the threatening environment of law enforcement administration.

Get Organized

You need your own space to work. You need an adequate filing system for memos, completed reports, blank forms, employee evaluation records, and a host of other administrative matters.

Failing to set up an adequate system of documentation, filing, and retention is guaranteed to make your life miserable at several points in the future. So make the commitment now to get organized for administrative survival. To assist you, ask your predecessor, one of your successful peers, or one of the secretaries. They should all be willing to contribute their expertise to increase your chances of survival.

Keep Good Records

Once you get organized, make a record and keep a record of everything you do, receive, send out, or handle. That may sound like a great deal of work, but you will quickly learn to handle it as a matter of routine.

Let's take a case of ammunition arriving at your precinct. Its arrival goes on the inventory record as being received and stored, and the paperwork with it is marked "received 2/12/10." File it in your "received" or an equivalent file. Should there be a question about whether or not it was received, the quantity received, or when it was received, you will have the answer and the documentation to prove it.

Write it Down

First, if it isn't on paper, it didn't happen. That includes employee counseling sessions, on-scene responses, and any other duty you perform. A simple, predated daybook, along with your handwritten entries, can be a big help in documenting your daily actions.

However, some actions require you to document the circumstances by report or memorandum, and that just goes with your new job. Accept it and do what you need to do to get them done right and on time.

Another reason to write everything down is so that you can remember it. With increased demands on your time and rapidly changing priorities, you have to write it down or it gets lost or forgotten, only to become a bigger problem later on. To avoid that happening, always write it down to remember to do it.

Develop Personal Contacts

When one of your officers claims that his paycheck is short, you can do a lot of paperwork to find out why, put it through channels, and wait to get a reply through channels. Your subordinate won't be happy with the delay, and the matter will be pending on your desk for a long time.

Wouldn't it be much easier if you could personally call up Sally in payroll and have her do a quick check of the records for you as a personal favor? No memos, no delays, and both you and your officer get the matter resolved quickly. Of course, you owe Sally lunch, but that's a lot better than all that paperwork and wasted time.

Manage Your Time

Unfortunately, promotions don't come with an expanded workday. There are still just eight hours in a shift and initially your increased responsibilities won't fit into that eight-hour day.

Not to worry. First, as you become more familiar with your new job, you will become more efficient. The end of the month reports that took you four hours the first time you did them will be reduced to much less time with experience.

Time will always be a pursuing monster unless you take charge of it. Getting organized will help. Developing personal contacts will help. What will help even more is to keep yourself from getting bogged down in minutiae or trivial matters. When subordinates try to lay their problems in your lap, reverse the momentum and point them in the right direction to solve their own problems.

Other hints include making use of quiet times, slightly before or after your regular shift. Also, limit visitors. There are times when it is necessary to spend time with people to solve problems, but when a solution is reached, end the interview. And of course, do the same with telephone calls and electronic messaging.

Time management is a critical and necessary task for a police supervisor to master. Successful time management is a matter of balancing employee needs against your needs, balancing on-scene supervision and administrative duties, setting realistic priorities, and allotting time to get them all done.

In the beginning, street survival will seem easy compared to your new world of administrative survival. However, the same effort and ingenuity that made you successful on the street will make you successful in your new assignment as a law enforcement administrator.

Section 2 — Getting a Handle on Your Time

With every promotion you receive comes an increase in the amount of duties and responsibilities you have to handle. Unfortunately, you don't get a corresponding increase in the number of hours in a day, nor extra days in the week, to handle that increased workload.

In order to meet their new challenges, many newly promoted officers will increase their workday, sometimes to as much as 12 to 16 hours a day, and will give the department an extra day or two a week, without any additional pay or benefits.

A better solution is to take charge of your new career. Look realistically at what duties you must perform on a daily basis. Then work smarter, and more efficiently, to get the work done in a reasonable amount of time.

From experience, here are a few common sense solutions to some of the biggest time-wasters in your workday. They may not solve all of your time-management problems, but they are guaranteed to make your work-week a little bit shorter.

Plan Ahead

If you know you have to plan a security detail for the 4th of July Parade, don't try to start it on the 3rd of July. If you do, you'll end up working all day, all night, and end up with poor performance at the parade.

Avoid those stress-filled, all night sessions by starting your planning early. That way, when little stumbling blocks fall in your way, you will have plenty of time to work them out before your deadline arrives.

Make Realistic Lists

You wouldn't even think about going on a drug raid without a well-thought-out plan. So why try to conduct the rest of your day without such a plan?

Writing out a to-do list for the next day, before you leave work, will allow you to go in, get focused on what needs to be done, and complete your required tasks on a priority basis.

Not only will you receive little confidence builders during the day as you scratch off completed tasks, but you will also feel good about accomplishing things when the list is exhausted and with time to spare at the end of the day.

Get Off the Telephone

It's a necessary part of life, but it can also be a real time-waster.

Learn to keep calls as short as possible, using a timer if necessary. Be cordial and polite, but get off the phone as soon as possible with people who don't seem to be as busy as you are. After all, if they want to work long days that's their business, but they aren't going to force you into the same game.

Limit Visitors

Once someone is in your office, it can sometimes be difficult to get them to leave, even when their business is completed. This includes your subordinates, the public, and anyone else who needs to speak with you.

The best way to handle the situation is to keep them out of your office in the first place. Whenever appropriate, meet them at the front desk, in the squad room, or another place where you have better control of when the meeting ends, because you will be the one leaving the scene.

Delegate

You are not the only person in the department who can solve problems. Train your subordinates how to handle recurring problems and encourage them to only bring problems to you if they cannot satisfactorily resolve them.

Use Quiet Times

Quiet times are those times when everyone else has gone home or has not arrived at work yet. These times allow you to work on projects without the usual interruptions.

Don't add quiet times to your workday! Schedule them as a part of your regular workday. You may want to start early, work late, or schedule a Sunday shift. Whatever your choice, these times are great for difficult projects.

There will always be time when unexpected field situations or administrative breakdowns will require you to work longer than normal hours. That usually goes along with a management position.

However, by following these few simple steps, you should be able to work smarter and more efficiently. That way, when these crises do occur, you will still have the energy to meet them head-on, solve them, and still get home in time to tuck the kids into bed.

Section 3 — Managing That Endless Line of Meetings

Every law enforcement administrator, from sergeant through chief, is called into meeting after meeting, both within their organization and with other agencies. They vary in size, intent and length, but nearly all of them have one thing in common: about 50% of the time spent in them is wasted.

Some meetings are routinely scheduled weekly or monthly, usually within the department. Still others are called by the chief, the mayor, the city manager, or some other organization that feels it must have your department represented. And, whether it is true or not, it seems that the more rank you have, the more meetings you must attend. Just ask any chief or sheriff.

Whether you are running these meetings, or just attending them, here are some tips to help you survive that endless line of meetings.

Is a Meeting Really Necessary?

With everyone's time at a premium, this is the first question to ask. The goal you hope to reach is the controlling factor here. What do you want to accomplish? Do you want to disseminate information, get input from a variety of sources, or do you want to sell an idea or program.

Next ask, "Is a meeting the best way to accomplish this goal, or would another method be just as good or better?" If the same or better results can be obtained by making a few phone calls, sending a few memos, an e-mail, or a few face-to-face meetings, then a meeting may not be necessary. Always try to find a reasonable alternative if possible.

Who Should Attend the Meeting?

Most chiefs and sheriffs are torn between so many people wanting them to attend one meeting or another that they have little time to run their organizations. Many of those meetings are necessary, and may require a police representative, but not necessarily the chief or sheriff.

As an example, your local planning committee sends a letter requesting that the chief attend a developer's presentation on a new shopping center. The chief could go and sit through a boring three-hour presentation, which would mostly affect other governmental functions. Or, a quick telephone call to the president of the planning board may reveal that all they need is a representative to listen to the proposed changes in the traffic-flow pattern. Once the purpose is known, the chief can assign it to the captain in charge of traffic, and the chief can enjoy his dinner at home that evening. The captain can go for the portion of the meeting dealing with traffic, and then he/she also can leave.

Set Out and Review the Agenda

If you are calling the meeting, be sure to set out a detailed agenda of what is to be discussed, and what you expect to accomplish. Send the agenda out in advance, so everyone can decide if they should go themselves, or who would be better to send. The agenda will help those attending to prepare to discuss the issues being addressed at the meeting. If you are an invitee, you should review the agenda for the same reasons.

Also, when writing or reviewing the agenda, be sure to note the starting and finishing times so everyone can plan other activities before and after the meeting.

Start on Time

Organized, competent professionals are where they should be, when they are supposed to be there. Don't penalize them for being on time by waiting for those who just can't seem to "get it together."

The disorganized one may be disruptive when entering the meeting for the first time. Once some gentle chiding makes it clear to them that meetings will start on time, with them there on time, there should be no further problem.

Limit Interruptions

Barring a major earthquake or equivalent natural or manmade disaster, all participants should plan to have a subordinate cover their calls to limit any interruptions during the meeting.

Inevitably, as soon as a key person leaves the meeting to answer a phone call, their input will be needed for the meeting to progress. The subsequent delay to all of the other attendees is unacceptable.

Stick to the Agenda

Keeping the goals of the meeting in mind, stay as close to the scheduled agenda as possible. This means both with regard to topic and time. As the moderator, this is your responsibility.

Don't allow others, with a self-serving or hidden agenda, to bog down the meeting with excessive talk, unrelated material, or disruptive behavior. Keep in mind that you are running the meeting, not the participants. Use tact initially to refocus the meeting. If that fails, be more assertive by firmly restating the purpose and goals of the meeting.

Summarize Results

When key points appear to be agreed on, restate them and ask for any further concerns. A simple statement such as, "What I am hearing is that we are in agreement regarding .... Is that correct?"

Given no strong objections, direct the person taking the minutes of the meeting to write down the terms of the agreement and move on to the next segment. At the end of the meeting, summarize all the points of agreement, clearly indicate who has agreed on, or been assigned to, future tasks, and be sure it is all written down in the minutes.

End the Meeting on Time

This is a measure of your credibility and competence. If the meeting doesn't end at the scheduled time, you will have upset the schedules of everyone at the meeting. It may also upset the schedules of a number of people who aren't even at the meeting who relied on your word that the meeting would end at a specific time.

It is also a measure of your ability to effectively plan, run, and control a meeting. If you can't run a simple meeting and get it done right, some may wonder what you can do right.

Meetings will always be a part of our lives. Even with the new technology allowing conference calls and video conferences, the rules aren't likely to change much. You still need the same skills to plan and run an efficient and productive hi-tech meeting as you needed for the ones in the old conference room.

Section 4 — Handling Information Overload

The information sources for a law enforcement professional are almost unlimited. There are the morning newspaper, morning news shows, and the radio news on the way to work. Then, once at work, there is that deep in-basket of police administration reports, memos, meetings, and e-mails. Add to it the law enforcement-oriented magazines, books, and government reports and your "information pile" becomes a daunting foe to defeat. Also add to it the resources of the Internet, and it's enough to put even the most dedicated commander over the edge into "Information Overload."

How can you survive in this sea of information, gleaning only what you really need? Here are a few tips for handling the glut of information crossing your desk and your brain day after day.

Evaluate Your Sources

Determine which of your sources provides you with the most relevant information for your position. The national news is nice to know, but for a city or county police commander, the local news may be much more valuable. There are dozens, if not hundreds of police newsletters and magazines available, but you only need to read those that provide you with information for your position.

Be Selective

Filter out the "critical" information from the "interesting" information. You may need to know about the Supreme Court decisions that affect law enforcement operations, but you don't need to wade through every Supreme Court decision. Therefore, you need a publication that specializes in law enforcement issues, not a general Supreme Court regaling publication.

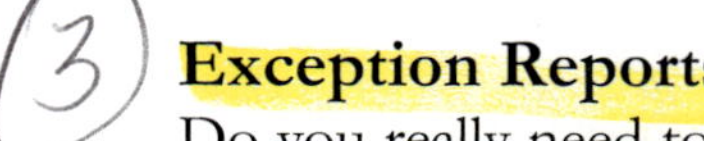

Exception Reports

Do you really need to know the gas mileage of every police car in your command? Of course not. What you need to know about is the police car that is getting far more or far less mileage than the average car. Therefore, you need an exception report, not a lengthy numbers report. Often, your computer people will be happy to provide such exception reports as opposed to giving you that huge general report. It saves them time and money with the same positive results for both of you. Talk to them.

Executive Summaries

Many lengthy reports, including government reports, have an executive summary at the beginning. Most police commanders need to know the conclusions of a study, not the methodology and all of the boring and time-consuming details. Read the executive summary only. If you question the findings, then delve deeper into the report. However, in most cases, the conclusions are all you need.

Delegate

President Dwight D. Eisenhower reportedly hated to read. Although he constantly received lengthy government volumes, he had a solution for handling them. Based on their titles, he would distribute them to the respective cabinet members with the phrase, "Please read this and let me know if there is anything in it that I need to know."

This strategy worked for him and it may also work for you. When you encounter an article or report on K-9 operations, you can read it, and/or give it to the head of your K-9 Unit with President Eisenhower's directive phrase. The same goes for many of the other specialized reports that may cross your desk on a regular basis. Of course, you need to have a good working knowledge of your command's units and trusted subordinates to use this technique.

The Internet

With millions of websites, tens of thousands of mailing lists and an additional tens of thousands of other groups, chat rooms, and blogs out there in Cyberspace, the filtering of these information sources is critical for any administrator. You have your own internal e-mail system to contend with. Therefore, the addition of outside information, although of great potential value, must be controlled. So, you need to be highly selective in what information you routinely receive on your Internet connection. Once again, you need to be highly selective in regarding the information sources you choose, as well as using your delegation powers to more efficiently direct the available information.

Be Brutal

Whether the task is filtering junk mail or directing unit-specific information to specific unit commanders, you must take control of the influx of information to your desk. The alternative is for you to work long hours receiving information that is better suited for others in the department, with little or no substantive increase in your knowledge or your ability to command.

The glut of information promises to worsen as we get further into the twenty-first century. Those law enforcement commanders who can effectively adapt and control information resources will blossom and grow. Those who become overwhelmed by information overload will retire in frustration.

The choice is yours!

Section 5 — Delegate — But Do It Right!

Do you have too much work and too little time? You are not alone! Administrators from sergeant through chief of police all have the same complaint. However, the smart ones are finding a solution to the time crunch right in their own organizations.

Much of what creates your time crunch is work that could just as easily be done by someone of a lesser rank. Even when a project requires your expertise or judgment, there may be background work that can easily be done by someone else. The proper delegation of some of these tasks can get the work done faster, help to develop and teach subordinates, and get you out of your acute time crunch.

Here are a few hints to help you delegate more effectively:

Decide what can be delegated

In general, the following areas can be *delegated:*

- Recurring problems that have routine solutions (scheduling problems, procedural problems)
- Routine matters (reports, inventories, maintenance)
- Time-consuming tasks (studies, statistical reports)
- Jobs you aren't good at (projects in specialty areas)

Do not delegate:

- Disciplinary power
- Policy-making issues
- Management functions specific to your rank (required approvals, monetary decisions, etc.)

Select the Right Subordinate

Be sure the employee you select has the knowledge, the experience, and the temperament to do the job. Also, be sure that the employee has the time and the willingness to get the work done by the deadline.

Communicate Well

Define the task well. Give exact details of what you want, how it should be done, and the results you expect. Set out the time constraints for the project. Then, be sure to give them the authority they need to get the job done.

Control and Follow-Up

Set up formal reporting times so that you can both discuss the status of the project and answer any questions. Check the work more closely in the beginning to be sure it is heading in the right direction. Overall, allow the subordinate freedom enough to complete the task as that person sees fit. However, remember that good follow-up is absolutely necessary for successful delegation.

Delegating work does not mean dumping all of your work on your subordinates so that you can go play golf. Nor does it mean casting off only the work you don't want to do.

Delegation does mean giving meaningful work to subordinates so they will grow, so you will work more effectively, and so the organization can run more effectively.

Section 6 — Career Traps

There are certain things in the real world of law enforcement management that can cancel out all of your good preparations and intentions for becoming a successful leader. Some are common and a little common sense can avoid them. Still others are more subtle and need to be pointed out to upwardly mobile officers so that they can avoid them.

It is amazing how many police careers fail, and too often end, as a result of good people failing to avoid these simple career traps despite their simplicity.

AVOID:

➢ *Criticism of Others*

Openly criticizing your subordinates will ensure their contempt for you and result in counterproductive activities for you. Openly criticizing your supervisors is also a surefire way to stifle your future career opportunities. Keep your criticisms to yourself.

➢ *Second-Guessing*

This is also known as Monday-Morning Quarterbacking. Subordinates should be encouraged to make their own decisions at the time, place, and under the circumstances they were faced with in any given situation. It is incumbent upon their leader to support those decisions whenever possible, even if those decisions were less than perfect.

➢ *Blaming Others*

When in a position of leadership, everything that occurs is your responsibility, even the errors. Your job is to minimize the damage, correct the problem, and assure that it doesn't happen again. Placing blame on others shows you are a weak commander.

➢ *Overspecialization*

Being a police specialist, in the lab, K-9, SWAT, and other areas, can result in a very rewarding career. But specialists seldom become leaders of large units or departments. Leaders need a wide variety of skills and experiences to succeed. Overspecialization in one area tends to make a person a technician rather than a leader.

➢ *Arrogance*

Don't be caught up in the power and prestige of your position. You must always be willing to help your subordinates, even in the most mundane of tasks. In addition, you must always be available to your people. An arrogant attitude will make you unapproachable and will ultimately put you out of reach, out of touch, and isolated from what is really going on in your unit.

➢ *Conflicts of Interest*

Keep in mind that the appearance of a conflict of interest can be as damaging to your career as actual corruption. Avoid gratuities, special favors, and preferential treatment if you want to be considered an officer with integrity. As a test of your integrity, tell your people that they can do anything they see you doing. That will put the pressure on you to follow the rules you make and enforce.

➢ *Unsavory Characters*

Who are your friends and associates? Are they the kind of people that a professional law enforcement person should be associating with? Cultivate friends who have the same high ideals of honesty and integrity that you have, regardless of their professions, and you will be in good company.

➢ *Sexual Harassment*

In order to avoid sexual harassment, a police leader must know what constitutes sexual harassment in the workplace today. Ignoring the reality of sexual harassment in the workplace will clearly jeopardize your otherwise successful career. Know and understand the laws, your department policies, and your role and obligations regarding sexual harassment prevention in the workplace.

➢ *Gossip and Rumors*

Avoid gossip and control rumors. Even if your department doesn't have a policy regarding workplace rumors and gossip, understand that it is your responsibility to control your unit. You are responsible for the morale of your unit, and rumors and gossip tend to undermine morale. Truth is the anecdote for rumors, and gossip has no place in the workplace. It's your command, and you are in charge. Handle it!

➢ *Lying*

Whether it is intentional or unintentional, avoid lying to anyone, anytime. Your credibility as a police commander is always at stake. Be sure of your facts and your authority and be scrupulously honest. It will serve you well throughout your career. In fact, in repeated

surveys, employees have cited "honesty" as the number one attribute they want in a police commander.

There are many career traps, some of a general nature such as noted above, some specific to your department. Know about them and understand their nature. It's relatively easy for an intelligent, upwardly mobile officer to stay on track, but you must work at it. With a little work and common sense, you can avoid falling victim to the common traps that have ended so many police careers.

Chapter 8
Personnel Management

A competent leader can get efficient service from poor troops, while on the contrary, an incapable leader can demoralize the best troops.

— General John S. Pershing

Section 1 — New Commander Problems and Solutions

Section 2 — Motivating Your Officers

Section 3 — Don't Coddle Poor Performers

Section 4 — "You Made a Mistake"—How to Criticize Effectively

Section 5 — Preventing Insubordination

Section 6 — Preventing Corruption

Section 7 — Unions

Section 8 — Promoting Teamwork

Section 9 — Ten Critical Areas to Check in Your Department

Section 1 — New Commander Problems and Solutions

"Congratulations, Lieutenant. You are hereby promoted and assigned to the 7th Precinct as the commander of that unit. Good luck!"

These can be great words at the ceremony, but both the promoter and the promotee might be quite surprised at what newly appointed commanders will be facing when they get to those new commands. The term, "good luck!" can have great meaning when the preconceived ideas of becoming a new commander meet the realities of the job of the commander of a unit or precinct.

For the benefit of everyone involved in the department, and particularly those responsible for the success of a particular unit, some understanding of the problems of taking on a new command can help everyone to succeed. By understanding the problems new commanders will face, superior officers can better prepare new commanders for their new positions. At the same time, this information can help the new commanders face the realities of their new positions.

So, to help everyone involved, here are a few of the problems new commanders said they have faced. And, because we try to never present a problem without also presenting a possible or probable solution, we have given you some solutions as well.

New Command Problem #1

Unclear Policies

It is recognized that even the most professionally written policy and procedure manual can leave room for interpretation. And, interpreting the gray areas of such policies and procedures is the job of a local commander. However, new commanders have concerns about receiving backing and support for the interpretations they make on a daily basis.

Solution: Professional departments have extensive policy and procedure manuals to cover many routine matters. Candidates for promotion, at any rank, should be tested to ensure that they have studied and understand these policies and procedures. In addition, senior command staff should reassure new commanders that they will receive the backing and support they need when they make a field interpretation at the time and place and under the field circumstances they face.

New Command Problem #2

Lack of Direction

A new commander is promoted and sent to take over a new unit, but with little or no direction. What is the goal of their new unit? Are they to "keep the lid on" or reduce robberies by 10%? Too often they are left to their own ideas, which may or may not be consistent with senior management's goals.

Solution: Senior command staff, particularly those who will directly oversee and evaluate the performance of the newly promoted commander, should meet to discuss the mission and goals of the unit. Some agreement and consensus should be reached that is understood by both parties to provide direction and performance standards that the new commander should implement at his or her new command.

New Command Problem #3

Micro-Management by Superiors

New commanders often feel that they are not trusted by their superior officers. They feel their superior officers are meddling in their commands. Those same superior officers feel that they are lending guidance to the new commander. Who is right?

Solution: Both parties may have legitimate concerns. The solution here is a balancing act. When superior officers appoint a new unit commander, they have supposedly selected the best person for the position through an extensive selection process. When that is done, superior officers must give that individual the opportunity to prove that he or she can handle the job, and at the same time, give that person the opportunity to fail. However, the new commander, if he/she is worthy of the title, must be able to stand up to the bosses and say, "Sir, I need to have the freedom to run my own unit."

New Command Problem #4

Preconceived Notions vs. Realities of the Job

Promotional candidates prepare for promotion by studying laws, manuals, and procedures. They prepare for oral boards, assessment centers, and in-basket exercises. And they succeed in all of those and get promoted.

When they take over their new command, they get hit with a heave dose of reality. Their people don't necessarily respond to those management theories they studied. Subordinates don't know, understand, or care about the nuances of the policy or procedure manual. In addition, they often encounter an air of ambivalence from both subordinates and superiors. In short, they are confused by the realities of their new position.

Solution: A Field Training Officer Program helps new patrol officers gain their footing by placing them with a professional patrol officer for a period of time. It helps new officers meld the theories of the law and procedures with the stark realities of street life.

A similar program, either formal or informal, should be used to assimilate new command officers into their new positions. A new sergeant, before taking over his or her own squad, should be assigned to work with an experienced sergeant. A new lieutenant could use a stint with an experienced lieutenant to help him or her face the cold realities of being a unit or precinct commander.

There are many problems facing a newly promoted police commander. We have listed only a few. Many of these problems can find solutions even before the new commander reaches his or her particular command. Good senior officers help their commanders succeed. Not-so-good commanders only give them a chance to "sink or swim" in their new positions.

Where do you stand?

Section 2 — Don't Coddle Poor Performers

Nearly every command has them!

You can recognize them by the way they continually violate basic rules. They either can't, or won't, follow proper procedures. In addition, the quantity and quality of their work is far below that of the rest of the unit.

What can you do about such poor performers?

First, use every motivational tool you can think of to help bring their performance up to par. Give them all of the assistance and training they need to help them improve their performance.

Second, counsel them, coach them, and use every other positive, professional management technique available to help them.

However, after you have exhausted all of these options without realizing a dramatic improvement in their poor performance, you must take actions that may result in "other arrangements" for the poor performers.

Poor performers, by failing to respond to your efforts to assist them, have placed you in a position where you must take such action. Your failure to take such action under these circumstances could ruin your career and the effectiveness of your unit.

Here is what can happen if you repeatedly fail to take the actions necessary to eliminate poor performance in your command:

Morale Suffers

When the hard-working members of your command see individuals repeatedly getting away with rule violations and generally poor performance, they naturally question why they are working so hard and conforming to all of the rules. After all, isn't everyone getting paid the same?

If equal pay means equal work, then they may feel that they should quit working so hard and conform to the poor performers' work standard. After all, you are apparently willing to accept this poor standard.

You Lose Respect

The members of your command look to you for guidance and direction. When you repeatedly make good decisions and take appropriate actions, they learn to respect you.

However, the reverse is also true. If they perceive that you are unwilling, or afraid, to take action to correct a problem that is so obvious, they will lose respect for you as a commander. Once that respect is lost, it is difficult, and may be impossible, to regain.

Your effectiveness and credibility as a commander will be seriously damaged.

Your Problems Compound

The minor rule violations you ignored can quickly turn into major rule violations when it appears that you don't care. The results of such major rule violations can cause serious problems for you and your unit from the media and other investigative and watchdog agencies.

The poor quality and quantity of work you were willing to accept will result in decreased productivity and can ultimately render your unit ineffective in meeting its goals.

Such ineffectiveness is a clear reflection of your poor leadership. When it reaches that point, it will be time for your boss to make "other arrangements" for you.

To avoid such a downward spiral for your career, all you have to do is to take appropriate action when it needs to be taken.

Insist on a reasonable quantity of high quality work. Require adherence to established policies and procedures. Be sure that the members of your command understand the rules and then enforce them equally for all.

Maintaining high, but reasonable, standards will allow everyone in your command to know what is expected of them and to meet those standards. Individuals who choose not to maintain their performance at the expected levels are solely responsible for their own destiny, and "other arrangements" may be in their near future.

Section 4 — "You Made a Mistake" — How to Criticize Effectively

As a police commander, you will sometimes have to criticize the actions of someone in your command. How you do it may hold the key to whether or not your criticism will result in positive change or in counter-productive behavior and animosity toward you and the department.

There is nobody in your department who is perfect, including you. At some point, we all make mistakes. Recognizing this simple fact should help you relate to the individual that you, due to your position, must chastise for their mistake, judgment, or behavior.

Here are ten simple guidelines to help you when you must call in a subordinate to say, "You made a mistake."

Get the Facts

Until you have all the facts, you cannot determine that someone made a mistake. Don't take someone else's word until you are personally satisfied that something did go wrong and that the person responsible is the person you will be confronting. Remember the phrase "innocent until proven guilty"?

Criticize the Conduct, Not the Person

Identify the conduct that you find faulty. It was the conduct that caused the problem, not the person. Therefore, direct your criticism at the action, not the person.

Be Specific

Be sure that you address specific conduct at the date, time, and place it occurred.

A phrase such as, "You are always late with your reports," is not acceptable. A phrase such as, "You missed the April 20th deadline for your report," is much more acceptable.

Ask for an Explanation

"Sergeant, did you have a reason for missing this deadline?" gives them the opportunity to explain their side and reasons for their actions. This may add to the information you already have on the incident. Or it may just result in their giving you an unacceptable excuse for their conduct.

Either way, it will be good, because the person will have the opportunity to present their case. Then you can best determine your further course of action.

Can the Behavior be Changed?

The primary purpose of criticism is to prevent recurrence of the problem in the future. You should ask yourself, as well as the offender, if this problem can be prevented from happening in the future.

It may be that there were inadequate policies or procedures in the manual. Maybe inadequate training contributed to the problem. Whatever it was, be sure you take the necessary steps to prevent the problem in the future.

Say Something Positive

"I know you had a difficult situation that night that you would normally handle well ..." or "You are a good sergeant who I can normally depend on ..."

Positive openings such as these can be very helpful in reinforcing the overall worth of the individual to the department, while still allowing you to get to the specific problem area.

Get In, Get Out

Address the critical issue, professionally and directly. Say what you have to say, criticize as you must and get out of it. Don't belabor the point.

Reaffirm Your Support

Exit your interview on a positive note.

"Despite this problem, I still have faith in your abilities. Let's put this incident behind us both and move on."

Avoid Problems

Try not to raise your voice, get angry or use sarcasm during the interview. Choose your words carefully and comply with any department or union contract guidelines for such interviews.

The Golden Rule Applies

"Treat others as you want to be treated," is the final word. We will all find ourselves on the receiving end of criticism at one time or another. Keep that in mind.

Section 5 — Preventing Insubordination

Insubordination; the generic definition is "a failure to submit to a higher authority, mutinous, rebellious." In law enforcement, insubordination is roughly defined as a failure to obey a lawful and direct order from a supervisor. On the surface, it seems quite simple. The officer did or didn't do what he or she was told. The reality is quite different. What may appear as a simple case of insubordination can ultimately become a complex legal battle of definitions, circumstances, and opinions once a disciplinary action is filed. With the subsequent involvement of grievance boards, attorneys, hearing officers, or the court system, the once simple issue of insubordination can be a subject of hours of controversy and debate. The final outcome can be uncertain.

As with any aspect of personnel management, the professional police administrator and supervisor would do well to study the topic of insubordination in order to know the limits of their authority and how their actions, and the actions of their subordinates, may be viewed by those who will stand in judgment of the issues.

Here are a few tips for the active law enforcement supervisor on the issue of insubordination.

Insubordination is Serious

To effectively run a police department as a paramilitary entity, discipline is required. This is particularly important when issues specific to public safety are involved. Hearing officers and courts have clearly recognized that insubordination within the ranks of a police organization cannot be tolerated, particularly in life or death situations, and they will generally, wholeheartedly support the police commander and the department in such cases.

However, most cases of insubordination brought before such bodies do not address clear-cut, life or death public safety situations.  Most of the insubordination cases brought involve routine, day-to-day, supervisor/subordinate relations that are rule, policy, or procedural violations. Most of these routine problems also have an emotional or historical component as well.

Choose Your Battles Carefully

You are clearly in charge of your department, precinct, or unit. Your position as a commander clearly conveys that to everyone involved with you. That's nice, but leadership is action, not just position. Keep that in mind as you approach your subordinates with direct orders and directions. Understand that your actions and the actions of your subordinates will be judged not on the emotional considerations of the  original situation but only on the merits of the insubordination case as presented by the advocates and opposing entities.

In a riot situation, your orders must be followed immediately to prevent harm to your unit and the public. Contrast that with ordering someone to "Get into my office, now!" to discuss a late report.

In the first case, there is clearly an immediate public safety issue. In the second, there is a less critical issue. Rest assured that hearing boards and courts will recognize that difference.

What Are the Consequences?

When someone balks at one of your orders, you will immediately recognize it. However, before that initial defiant attitude rises to the level of insubordination, take a moment and think about where this tense situation might lead. Let the subordinate know that their failure to comply may result in disciplinary action. In essence, warn them that you are serious about this order.

If you know the degree to which the officers may be disciplined, make them aware of it. In critical situations, their refusal to obey may result in dismissal from the force. In less critical situations, the disciplinary action may result in reprimand, loss of vacation days, or suspension. Keep in mind that you rarely know exactly what will happen in the end.

Once an employee is put on notice of the possibility of disciplinary action and the potential consequences of their failure to perform, they may comply with your directions. If not, your position in future hearings will be greatly enhanced because of your notice.

Are You Part of the Problem?

Your authority is not absolute. If it was, you might be replaced by a robot or rule book. Supervision requires human judgment. That supposition also subjects the supervisory process to human frailties.

Personalities enter into the insubordination issue. In one case, a newly promoted sergeant brought charges of insubordination against an officer for failure to respond to a direct order to get into his office. When the charges reached the hearing officer, in this case the chief of police, the chief responded with, "You two didn't get along as patrolmen. Now go out there and get along. Case dismissed."

You can argue any side of the case, but you must also face reality. Some cases of "insubordination" stem from past issues, stubbornness, or lack of interest. The hearing officers and courts will take that into account if it gets that far.

Conclusion

The case law is clear. When there is a serious case of insubordination that could impact on public safety or the critical operational components of police department operations, hearing officers and the courts back police supervisors and managers. Conversely, when the issues of the cases involve minor or petty disagreements or attitudes, their decisions are decidedly less imposing on the defendants.

Keep in mind that most insubordinate cases do not ultimately result in termination, which means you may get that employee back again after the lengthy disciplinary process has only fined, suspended, or reinstated that employee. That can be when the battle really begins.

Choose your battles carefully. Every great and successful commander has done that.

Section 6 — Preventing Corruption

Call it by any name that fits the current situation being broadcast night after night on both the 6 o'clock and 11 o'clock news. It might be allegations of police corruption, scandal, abuse of power, allegations of criminal activity, or claims of brutality filed against a member of your department.

The allegations are bad enough, but if they are proven true, it can be devastating to the entire department—sometimes for years in the future. You might ask yourself: "How did it get to this point?"

The fact is that many incidents of police corruption and scandal can be prevented. It's not easy. It requires a great deal of effort and commitment from police leadership but most problems of this nature can be prevented. Here are a few tips to help you keep corruption and scandal out of your unit and your department.

Hire the Best

What is it that you want from your entry-level police officers? The answer may depend on the size of your department, the nature of your policing mission, the population that you are serving, and so on. The standards that you set for physical, mental, and psychological fitness (at entry-level and beyond) should reflect those policing goals.

Then find the best possible candidates who meet these criteria and actively recruit them into your department. Do not turn this function over to a bureaucratic general personnel department. Recruitment should be a police department's function. You know what you are looking for, you should know how to find the right people, and your best officers are natural role models for your new candidates.

Investigate, Investigate, Investigate ...

When police officers' careers crash into corruption and scandal, the media often finds some form of moral turpitude in their background *before* they ever became police officers. That kind of information should be caught by the original background investigators prior to hiring that officer A department needs to have a formal and detailed background investigation process in place. The department's *best* and most thorough investigators need to be assigned these background investigations. They need to be given the time and resources to complete these investigations. Too often departments move too quickly or ignore a thorough investigation entirely.

A better plan needs to be implemented so that proper and thorough background investigations can be done without rushing to meet artificial and counterproductive deadlines.

Avoid Outside Influences

When the standards are set and the background checks are done, there may be appeals from rejected candidates. Handle each one on its own merits. Some candidates will threaten lawsuits on their own, while others may appeal through local politicians or special interest groups. In some cases, a department's own personnel department will want to avoid controversy.

This is the time when police commanders must exhibit sound leadership responsibilities. They must stand up for the high standards and moral criteria they want in their department. To cave in to the avoid controversy lobbies or the whims of politicians who will be long-gone when a police scandal erupts in the future will ensure that controversy and corruption stories will continue to be broadcast across the televisions screens and newspapers of your community.

Promote Honesty and Integrity

Police commanders must exemplify the honesty and integrity they seek in their subordinates. Not only must they stand against undue political influence in hiring, they must exhibit integrity in every aspect of their daily activities.

Police commanders must also take action when necessary against minor transgressions by department personnel so that those personnel are put "on notice" that such conduct is not tolerated in the unit or the department. And police commanders, at all ranks, must insist that their personnel always do the right thing when dealing with the public, their own subordinates, and their peers.

Honesty and integrity, at all levels of your police department, are two of the most important traits you can exhibit to help prevent controversy and corruption within your department.

The public's trust is critical to the overall success of the mission of your department. You can't touch it or see it, but when you walk into a community, you can feel when it's there and when it's not. Without public trust, a police department is hollow and ineffective.

Section 7 — Unions

It might be called the Police Benevolent Association, or it might go by another name and be affiliated with a major trade union. The fact remains that it is a union. It was organized to protect the rights of its

members in the workplace and you, as a representative of management, must work within the guidelines set out in a negotiated contract.

Too many supervisors at all levels of police management don't fully understand their relationship with the unions, nor their obligations under the union/management contracts. Whether you are a sergeant, lieutenant, captain, or chief, you must work within the confines of the written contract. To be ignorant of its terms or to ignore them is to invite problems in your command and possibly cause serious harm to your career.

To effectively work with unions and avoid the pitfalls associated with such dealings, a few simple guidelines are offered to help keep your career on track.

Know the Contracts

Get copies of the contracts that cover all of your employees. Police officers may have one contract, and civilian employees may have their own. Lower-level supervisors may have a contract that is different from mid-level managers. Senior officers may not be covered by a union contract, but it's up to you to be sure.

Carefully read each contract and understand your duties and obligations and those of the employees in fulfilling each clause of the contract. Try to visualize each clause as an action in your daily routine. Then, when you are satisfied that you understand the meaning and intent of the clause, keep a copy of the contract where you can readily find it. Many grievances can be resolved quickly by a good supervisor "getting out the books" and settling the problem at the first sign of a disagreement.

Comply With the Contract

Whether you like the terms of the contract or not is immaterial. It is a negotiated, legally binding document and you must abide by its terms. If it requires certain procedures, you must follow them. If it prohibits particular conduct, such as discrimination for filing a past grievance, then you had better not discriminate.

Many grievances that are sustained are the result of managers and supervisors who have chosen to do it their way instead of doing it the way the contract requires. In reality, if you follow the rules and procedures set out in the contract, you will avoid most grievances in the first place and that saves everyone time and energy.

Treat Employees Fairly

Unions were started to protect employees against unfair and unreasonable actions of employers. Therefore, it follows that if you treat your employees fairly and with the respect they deserve, there will be no reason for the union to step in to contest your daily interactions with your employees.

Because most union representatives don't go looking for a confrontation, a violation must be called to their attention by an offended employee. They are usually required to then take some action to resolve the conflict.

Your relationship with your employees can be an important factor in whether or not they contact their union steward. If, in your good faith efforts to get a job done, you make a decision that technically violates a clause of the contract, your reputation as an otherwise fair and just supervisor may carry you through without any problem. Conversely, if you have a reputation for constantly trampling on your employees' rights, the steward's phone will ring loud and often, and so will yours.

Know the Steward

Whenever you take over a new command, get to know the stewards for the unions involved in your operation—before any disagreements occur. Let them know that you are interested in maintaining a good labor/management relationship, and that you are willing to resolve any problems to the satisfaction of everyone concerned.

Starting and maintaining such a relationship can pay big dividends down the road when problems occur. Nobody wants to spend endless hours in grievance hearings over disagreements that could have been resolved between two rational people at a much lower level. In fact, most grievances can be resolved quickly and easily if both sides talk with each other on a regular basis.

Follow the Grievance Procedure

If a grievance cannot be resolved at your level despite your best efforts, it must proceed to the next highest level of the grievance procedure. This generally includes issues beyond your control, or discrepancies in the interpretation of the terminology of the contract clause covering an issue.

You must understand that such problems do occur, and it is not a reflection on your leadership. Your only job is to ensure that you follow the proper procedures to get it to the next level. In addition to documenting your efforts to resolve the conflict, you must be sure that you comply with all of the time limits required in the contract. Once you meet your obligations, the resolution of the problem is out of your hands. In time, you will probably be advised of the outcome of the grievance by superiors so that such conflicts can be avoided or resolved at a lower level in the future.

Reasonable people who represent different interests involved in the same situation can occasionally disagree. The resulting grievances are not an attack on your personal integrity nor on your leadership ability. They are a routine part of the labor/management relationship and are designed to resolve conflicts in a reasonable and orderly fashion.

Understanding your role in labor/management conflicts can help you to prepare for and avoid conflicts, resolve them quickly when you can, and allow you to properly handle those conflicts that can only be resolved at a higher level.

Section 8 — Promoting Teamwork

Having a bunch of talented players is not the only key to having a successful team. Those talented players need a talented coach to give them guidance, maintain discipline, and promote the goals and objectives of the organization. In short, they need a team leader.

In police work, that team leader would be you as a unit or departmental commander.

To help you promote teamwork in your particular unit, here are a few simple tips to help you succeed.

Care About Your People

You are the commander of a unit, but that unit is made up of human beings. Each one of your people is an individual, with individual needs, goals, and concerns. Each one looks to you for guidance, leadership, and respect. Respect is a two-way street. Be sure to respect your people, concern yourself with their needs and welfare, and they will respond in kind.

Tell Them What You Want

In any industry, most employees want to please the boss. But too often the boss doesn't tell the employee what the goals are, what the policies are, or what procedures they need to follow to perform their job satisfactorily. Yes, the policy and procedure manual can help, but tell your people what you want from them. They can't give it to you if they aren't sure what you want.

Get Everyone's Input

Most command decisions are of a routine nature. Therefore, you have the time to solicit input from your people. Novice commanders don't do this. Experienced commanders know that their people want to be heard and want input into command decisions. Therefore, take the time to solicit input and listen to your people's concerns and opinions. The final decision will be your responsibility, but your people will be happy that they had input even if your decision doesn't go their way.

Promote the Team

Your unit or department will not be successful as an independent entity. It requires that a whole team of people pull together in a single, concerted effort to attain a common goal. That is true whether you have a five-person unit or a 500-person unit. Everyone needs to contribute to the team if the team is to be successful. Promote the team effort among all of your people and emphasize that individual excellence translates into team success.

Be the Team Captain

Regardless of your actual rank in your unit, you need to be the leader of your team. Every team needs a leader and that would be your job. Do what any team captain would do: direct, envision, and work with every person on your team to pursue the objective to work hard and be the best they can be while contributing to the overall objective.

Hold Them Accountable

A team's efforts can be thwarted by the poor performance of one or more poor performers. You cannot tolerate poor performers if you are to have a successful team for your unit or department. You will need to work with any poor performers you might have on your team to improve their performance to make them an integral part of the team or to encourage them to work harder for the team. But if they choose to continue to be poor performers, they need to go elsewhere or have other arrangements made for them. This is a decision they have made by their substandard performance.

Successful teams, whether in sports or law enforcement, don't just happen. Success is a caused event by the coach, sergeant or chief who nurtures and respects his/her people and demands high standards of performance.

How do you stack up as the coach of your team?

Section 9 — Ten Critical Areas to Check in Your Department

Training for police department management personnel varies widely among departments. Although some departments provide no training for anyone above the rank of patrolman, more progressive departments provide a comprehensive management development program for everyone from sergeant to captain.

To help you evaluate the management training program in your department, ten of the most common problem areas are discussed in this section. If any of these problems exist within your department, it may be time for your training staff to take corrective action.

1. ***Failure to Train Managers*** – Currently, there are only a few states that require a police department manager to attend any form of management training program. However, most professional departments recognize the need for adequate training for their managers and provide such training without an outside mandate.

Providing an adequate management training program results in better managers with a minimum of personnel, union, and operational problems, which is good for everyone from patrolman to chief.

2. ***Failure to Train Before Assignment*** – Even when a department requires training, the requirement is usually phrased, "must attend training within one year of promotion." Almost invariably, the phrase is translated "must attend training within one year *after* promotion."

Therefore, newly promoted managers are thrust into their new positions prior to any training. They are expected to perform their duties properly, although they aren't told what their duties are or how to perform them.

If they are lucky, they get by without making a critical error. If they aren't so lucky, they can ruin their career and personal reputation.

Training department managers before they are promoted prepares them for their new duties and relieves a great deal of their stress, which results in fewer problems for the department.

3. ***Failure to Evaluate Training Needs*** – The critical question is, "What do your police department managers need to know to adequately perform their duties?"

   Although a police manager's duties are similar from department to department, they are not identical. Therefore, it is critical to conduct some form of "needs assessment" specifically within your department.

   A formal needs assessment conducted by an independent consultant is ideal. However, if your department doesn't have the resources to conduct such a detailed study, there are still some steps you can take to identify your training needs. Some of these include surveys of incumbents, detailed examination of job descriptions, conferring with other departments, and the use of consultants for guidance on a limited basis.

4. ***Failure to Provide Specialized Training*** – All police department managers were created equal, but they didn't stay that way. Every manager brings unique skills, talents and experiences to their new position. Conversely, these unique skills, talents and experiences may also result in knowledge and experience gaps.

   Take for example the patrol sergeant whose new duties as a lieutenant include leadership of the SWAT Team, although no formal training in antiterrorist weapons or tactics has taken place. Less dramatic is the newly promoted administrative captain who must prepare the department's annual budget with no idea of where to begin.

   Although the specialized knowledge problem is most likely to occur in a large department, the training staff in every department should be alert to such problems. When a promotion is anticipated, they should ensure that the candidate has, or soon receives, all the training required for the new position.

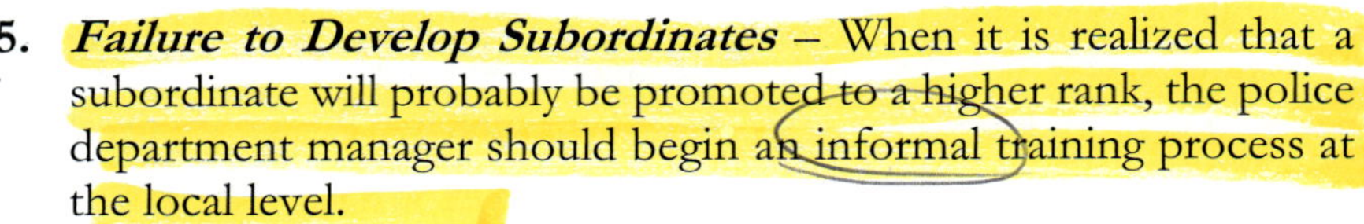

5. ***Failure to Develop Subordinates*** – When it is realized that a subordinate will probably be promoted to a higher rank, the police department manager should begin an informal training process at the local level.

Gradually increasing subordinates' involvement and responsibility will help prepare them for their new position. In some departments, this is done informally. Others may require it to be addressed as a formal part of the training process. Regardless of how it is done, it should be part of the training process in your department.

6. ***Failure to Provide Field Training for Managers*** – Perhaps the best training an individual can receive is practical, hands-on training from an experienced incumbent. Yet, field training programs seldom exist beyond the recruit training level.

A newly promoted person at every rank should have the opportunity to learn the practical side of their new position from a seasoned veteran before being thrust into a command position.

7. ***Failure to Provide In-Service Training*** – Many departments, even if they provide basic training for their managers, fail to provide any form of in-service training. Too often, the only time such training occurs is when the chief or sheriff wants to tell everybody something and calls all the supervisors into the same place at the same time.

That's a start, but laws, policies, procedures, and technology are continually changing. New human resource techniques are constantly being developed that managers can use to keep their subordinates motivated and happy. In addition, their old skills can become rusty or in need of rejuvenation.

A sound and regularly scheduled in-service program that presents information to update and upgrade managers' skills should be a part of every department's management training program.

8. ***Failure to Train Managers in What Subordinates Are Learning*** – Managers cannot know the full capabilities of their staff, unless they know the subjects their staff is trained in, and the procedures they are trained to follow, and the full extent of their training.

Imagine a manager arriving at the scene of a high-risk felony stop conducted by patrol officers, with no knowledge of the procedures taught in the officers' "Street Survival" course—a dangerous scenario at best.

Although most situations are less dramatic, the need to make managers aware of their subordinates' training programs is important but often overlooked by those designing the training programs.

9. ***Failure to Require Attendance at Training Programs*** – It boils down to priorities. A lieutenant is scheduled for in-service training. While en route to the academy, he is notified of a hostage situation in his sector. He immediately goes to the scene and takes charge of the situation for several hours.

Even if managers make it to class, the endless phone calls, emergency meetings, and critical incidents can ruin the best of training programs.

Departments must make it clear that training is as important as any other activity and demand their managers attend. If an emergency takes them away, they should be required to attend at a later date.

How ironic if the lieutenant who went to the hostage situation had been scheduled to attend classes on "Effective Delegation" and "How to Trust Subordinates."

10. ***Failure to Use Adequate/Certified Instructors*** – Good management instructors can be hard to find. Locating instructors who have the education, training, and experience in the police management field can be difficult, particularly when needed to train lieutenants and captains.

However, it is absolutely necessary for training personnel to expend the time, effort, and money to seek out the best possible instructors. Not only is the credibility of the instruction at stake, but the future of your department relies on the proper training of your management team.

Departments should not underestimate the long-term value of providing a comprehensive and continuing management development program for their managers.  The proper training of managers is critical to building and maintaining a strong and professional police department.

Chapter 9

LEADING THE WAY!

Management is doing things right—leadership is doing the right thing.

— Peter Drucker

Section 1 — What is Leadership?

Section 2 — The Will to Lead

Section 3 — What is a Leader?

Section 4 — What Leaders Do that Managers Don't

Section 5 — Supervising Your Subordinates

Section 6 — Specialty Units — Getting Them to Work Together

Section 7 — Department Culture — What's Yours Like?

Section 1 — What Is Leadership?

President and World War II Commanding General Dwight D. Eisenhower offered his own definition of leadership:

> *"Leadership: The art of getting someone else to do something you want done, because he wants to do it."*

President Eisenhower's definition of leadership is valid, but it addresses only the end result of successful leadership. Because those of us in law enforcement aren't as experienced as General or President Eisenhower, perhaps we need to look at the more basic, or interim, components of successful leadership.

In order to become a successful leader, it is necessary to prepare to be a leader. Earlier in this book, we advised you on preparation, promotion, and promotability. We have also presented traits and attributes that can help and may be necessary to your ability to become a successful leader.

This particular section is presented to bridge the gap between the preparation for leadership and the final result. To that end, the critical step of understanding the concept of leadership is presented here.

Vision

If you climb a tower, the higher you go, the more you can see on the horizon. That analogy holds true for climbing the ranks of a law enforcement organization as well. The higher you go in rank, the more you can see of the organization and its goals.

For those upwardly mobile officers who have prepared themselves accordingly, their elevation to a higher rank gives them insight into where the organization is and where it is going. Those astute officers develop a vision of where their unit or organization should be in the future. That vision is a necessary component for successful leadership.

Formulating the Plan

It is not enough just to know what a professional law enforcement organization looks like based on your education, training, and experience. Successful leaders evaluate their organization's current position, compare it to their vision of a highly effective, modern, and progressive police organization, and then they formulate a plan to reach that goal.

At this point, leaders stand out from their lesser peers. Although others point to budgeting problems, manpower shortages, and political impediments, true police leaders look for, and find, solutions to all of these problems. Not only are these leaders thoughtful and positive, but they proceed forward as men and women of action, not merely of the position or rank they have been assigned. Rank, without action, is *not* leadership.

Sharing the Vision

Action is what separates the contemplative police thinker from the effective police leader. It is not enough to devise a great plan for a professional police organization—that plan must be shared with the other members of the organization. At this stage, successful leaders share their vision, and they create an atmosphere of enthusiasm and excitement about the future goals of their unit, command, or department.

Successful leaders use a variety of tactics to promote their vision of a great and effective organization to its members. Their tactics include gaining the confidence, respect, and loyalty of both their subordinates and superiors. Once the leader's credibility is clearly established, he or she can share their vision openly with their members. Having done this, the effective leader can move on to the next stage of the leadership formula.

Developing Commitment

No matter how prepared, competent, and insightful a leader is in any organization, he or she cannot succeed alone. Successful law enforcement leadership requires the actions and commitment of dozens, hundreds, or even thousands of individual department members, from a wide variety of units and positions.

A true leader recognizes the absolute necessity of this action step. The leader then works at all levels of his or her organization to enlist the support and enthusiasm of all toward the accomplishment of the final goal of excellence in policing. He or she recognizes the diversity of all of the units involved, works through their sometimes competing agendas, and brings them together for the common goal in order to fulfill the vision.

Is this whole process of leadership easy? No!

Do leaders face constant challenges at all levels of the leadership process? Yes!

Then why do it? The answer is simple. It's the right thing to do if you are a true leader who is committed to the goal of excellence for your department.

And you will be in good company with General and President Eisenhower and the many other successful leaders who have shown you the way to attain the status of a truly successful leader.

It's worth getting there!

Section 2 — The Will to Lead

The young officer thought his journey was over. He had worked hard to get his education. He had studied hard for the exam. And he certainly showed that oral board that he knew how to play their game. He got the promotion and the big pay raise.

Then everything went flat. The men and women in his command kept their distance. They didn't seem to be enthusiastic about their work. They went through the motions, morale was down, and sick leave was up.

The new commander didn't fare much better. He never really felt comfortable. He was seldom sure of his decisions. Maybe another training course would help … maybe more experience … maybe more time … .

The truth is there was a missing piece in this officer's success puzzle from the beginning. The young officer's motivation and preparation was for the promotion process, not for the promotion. He was lacking the number one requirement for success in a leadership position—the will to lead.

There is no substitution for the will to lead others. Successful leaders, at any rank or position, must have the will to lead; the will to make things happen and the will to command and control people, equipment, and events. As Field Marshal Viscount Slim, a distinguished World War II British commander stated, "You cannot be a leader at all without this strength of will, this determination."

The commander of any unit must want to be in charge; must want to solve problems and resolve situations; and must want to take the responsibility for the actions of the people they lead.

The officer who aspires to a command position merely for the increased pay, benefits, and prestige, is likely to find the prestige portion missing very quickly. Without the will to lead, he and his unit will be doomed to mediocrity at best, and possibly the complete failure of their assigned mission. Such is the fate that a weak-willed commander inspires.

Successful commanders prepare for their positions very much like the young officer in our opening scenario. However, the successful commander's defining characteristic is his or her will to command and lead.

Perhaps legendary football coach Vince Lombardi put it best when he said, "The difference between a successful person and others is not a lack of strength, not a lack of knowledge, but rather in a lack of will."

When our young officer develops that will to command and lead, then he and his unit will finally be successful.

Section 3 — What is a Leader?

The traits of successful leaders have been studied repeatedly. Although there is not an exact consensus of all the attributes a leader needs to succeed, there are some traits that nearly all leaders possess.

Honesty

Repeated surveys have shown that people want leaders who are honest. In most surveys, honesty ranks number 1 on the list.

Peers, subordinates, and bosses respect and trust honest leaders.

Confidence

True leaders maintain a calm, internal confidence because they have worked hard, prepared for the tough situations, and have built on both their past successes and their occasional failures.

Humility

Leaders live for success, yet they need to be humble about their successes. True leaders simply say: "Thank you" for compliments, and they always give credit for their successes to their subordinates.

Leaders have egos, but they keep them in check.

Optimism

For true leaders, each new day presents challenges to meet and conquer. They maintain a positive "can do" attitude that they naturally convey to their subordinates.

Those leaders know how to develop new and innovative solutions to any problem they encounter.

Energy

Leaders must have a strong personal energy. That energy is what allows them to rise to challenges, take on difficult projects, and see them through to a successful conclusion.

Vision

Leaders see the future, not with a crystal ball, but with their knowledge of what the objective is, what it will take to get their unit there, and what each person's role is in fulfilling the mission.

At all levels, true leaders must have a vision of the future that they share with their people.

Courage

Both physically and morally, leaders must have the courage to move forward. They must have the courage to go where others fear to go. They must have the courage to face adversity, to support and protect their people. And they must occasionally have the courage to stand up to their superiors when necessary.

Loyalty

Leaders are loyal to their subordinates, to their bosses, to their organization and to their community.

Blind loyalty is not acceptable behavior for a leader. However, true loyalty can mean constructive disagreement with a boss or a subordinate for the good of all.

Adaptive

True leaders welcome change. Leaders ensure that others, subordinates and bosses alike, see the need to change or adjust and help them through that transition.

Leaders build flexibility into their plans to allow for unexpected changes, and they are always willing to make changes when warranted.

Tenacity

Leaders don't give up. They keep striving toward success until it is obtained. Ultimately, their tenacity will endure and their vision will be realized.

There are many traits that leaders need to be successful. The preceding ten traits are some of the most recognized. Aspire to them—the effort will serve you well!

Section 4 — What Leaders Do That Managers Don't

It has been said that "Managers do what is right, but leaders do the right thing." Is there a difference between being a manager and being a leader? You bet there is!

Here are a few things that those who earn the title of "leader" do that some law enforcement managers haven't quite figured out yet.

Leaders Assume the Leadership Role

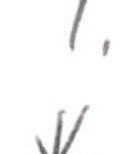

Just being placed in charge of a unit doesn't automatically mean you can lead it. You must, after being promoted, take charge and begin leading. A leader who understands his or her role and who has the knowledge, ability, and the will to lead will quickly be seen as the person in charge. People want to be led by a strong and competent leader. Assuming the leadership role by giving your people direction and purpose will help them perform individually and as a cohesive unit.

Leaders Think in Terms of Solutions

Leaders understand that problems are inevitable annoyances of life and police work. Where the manager frets and places blame, the leader takes immediate steps to solve the problem and to minimize the damage. After the immediate problem is solved, the leader takes steps to ensure that the problem doesn't recur. Then the entire unit moves on to bigger and more important accomplishments.

Leaders Surround Themselves with Competence

In addition to being competent themselves, leaders seek out the best qualified, most progressive associates they can find and develop them. Where managers may be afraid of such bright and energetic people taking their jobs, leaders welcome such close associates to their team so that everyone can maximize their potential. A true leader is secure enough in his or her abilities to help develop future leaders in their commands. That ultimately helps everyone get promoted, as well as meeting or exceeding the unit's operational goals.

Leaders Take Calculated Risks

Risk-taking is the arena where it is easy to distinguish between the safety-seeking managers and the more risk-taking leaders. Leaders are more willing to speak out in the heat of controversy. They are more willing to go to bat for their subordinates. Leaders dare to try new and innovative ideas, sure in their own minds of what will work and aware of the risks involved. Leaders do not risk the safety of their subordinates or someone else's career, but they are willing to take reasonable risks with their own careers.

Leaders Take Responsibility

True leaders take charge and responsibility for every facet of their operation. When things go well, they point to their unit and say, "They did well." When things don't go so well, they take the responsibility for the failure and vow to move forward despite the problems. Then they get to work once again to make the unit's next operation successful.

Leaders Always Move Forward

Leaders are always moving forward toward their objectives and goals. Sometimes the progress is slow. And sometimes they suffer temporary setbacks, but their overall momentum, for them and their unit, is forward. Their units are the first to try new policies, procedures, and technologies. They doggedly push their units to be the best they can be, with all the pride associated with being the best. The leader's and the unit's efforts ultimately lead to successful operations at all levels.

Leaders Lead by Example

Subordinates take their lead from their leader. They will emulate, consciously or subconsciously, the conduct and values they see in their commander. If you are forward-thinking, innovative, progressive, and professional as a leader, then your officers will likely follow your lead. Your commitment and dedication to the ideals of police work and the fulfillment of your unit's mission will be infectious and your entire unit will be positively affected by your actions. True leaders are excellent role models.

Leaders Have Vision

True leaders are able to visualize the goals of the unit and the steps necessary to reach those goals. They understand the rewards of success and the consequences of failure. The leader's vision defines the final goal and the leader's actions define the path to that goal. But despite the leader's vision and understanding, they must go further. They must be able to articulate and share their vision with their subordinates. In sharing their vision, they must be able to "excite" their subordinates about working toward those goals and the associated rewards. Once the goal and rewards are understood, subordinates will willingly work diligently to reach the goals and ultimately obtain the rewards of success for themselves and their unit.

Caution

Although the principles of leadership are consistent over time, the ability to lead is an ability sought by many but achieved by few. Being a successful leader in law enforcement requires many skills and abilities, and leadership can be as risky as it is rewarding. However, the satisfaction of being a true leader far exceeds the safety of being a mediocre manager. Go ahead and dare to enjoy the rewards of being a successful leader at any rank throughout your police career.

Section 5 — Supervising Your Supervisors

As any good law enforcement administrator knows, one of the keys to success is to surround yourself with good people. Those people should be technically competent, extremely dependable, and loyal to you and the department. Having those attributes is not always enough, however, for them to be successful police supervisors.

Because their responsibilities involve supervising the work of others, they must work well with their subordinates. They must avoid the common mistakes often made by supervisors when dealing with their people in order to keep their operations running smoothly

You must, as the "supervisor of your supervisors," watch for signals at an early stage that can help you identify problems at one of your units. The prompt identification of problems, and subsequent remedial action on your part, can prevent an otherwise smooth operation from developing serious problems due to supervisory errors. By properly monitoring your supervisors and intervening only when absolutely necessary, you can help your supervisors grow and develop without having them make unnecessary career-ending errors.

The following common mistakes are most often committed by

people who have not had previous supervisory experience. However,

experienced personnel taking over new operations can also make some of these common mistakes.

Failure to Take Charge

Newly appointed supervisors often fail to make the transition from worker to manager. They continue to try to be one of the guys. Initially they may not fully understand they must take charge of the unit to give it direction and discipline. Even experienced supervisors may fail to deal with personnel problems, and may even do subordinates' work for them to keep up the appearance that the operation is running smoothly.

Repeated studies have shown that the individual who assumes the leadership role—by confronting and solving problems—has the greatest chance of succeeding. Supervisors who do not assume that role may survive in the short run, but their abdication of responsibility will ultimately result in poor performance and internal chaos in their operation.

Help your supervisors avoid these problems by ensuring they understand their role as a supervisor and a leader *before* they take over a unit.

Failure to Maintain Good Morale

High morale in any organization ensures that people enjoy their working atmosphere and it allows them to work at peak efficiency. The supervisor who is insensitive to the factors that contribute to good morale is doomed to fail. Doling out only negative criticism, failing to recognize subordinates' achievements, playing favorites, treating employees unfairly or without respect can all lead—individually or collectively—to poor morale within a unit.

On the positive side, a competent supervisor treats his people fairly, keeps them informed, encourages dialogue, and shares the unit's successes with them. He treats everyone with dignity and respect and is reasonable in all interactions with them. He works at building a team—the best team in the business. Good morale is a natural byproduct of these actions.

You can help prevent morale problems in your units by ensuring that your new supervisors understand that they are the single greatest influence on morale in their unit. They also need to understand that subordinates of excellent leaders have excellent morale.

Failure to Make Proper Decisions

When a supervisor fails to make timely decisions that affect their subordinates, the result is a lack of direction for the work and a loss of confidence in the supervisor. Late or inconsistent decisions are almost as damaging as no decision.

On the other hand, a supervisor who continually exceeds his/her authority can also adversely affect law enforcement administration, can cause interdepartmental problems, and can jeopardize the overall mission of the department.

Your role in helping your subordinates make proper decisions is to clearly delineate the supervisor's duties and areas of responsibility, both verbally and in writing. Also, you need to give them continuing assurance that you will support their decisions whenever their decisions are reasonable, based on the facts and circumstances at the time and place they had to make the decision, even if it was less than perfect. This will give them the confidence to make timely and proper decisions in the future, without excessive guidance from you.

Your ability to continually monitor and evaluate the performance of the supervisors under your command is critical to your success and to the success of the units under your command. Your intervention at a critical point, without meddling in everyday operations, can be instrumental in keeping your units running smoothly.

Being aware of the potential problems listed above is the first step to success. The timing of your intervention is a matter of good judgment on your part. But then that's part of keeping up the morale of all of your subordinates. Are you up to the challenge?

Section 6 — Specialty Units — Getting Them to Work Together

It's not usually intentional. Many times the commanders don't even realize that the uniformed patrol force and the detectives seldom talk to each other. The commander of the SWAT unit doesn't know much about detective operations, and uniformed personnel have not all been trained in how to protect a crime scene for the K-9 unit. Yet each unit could, and should, learn a great deal from the other units.

To ensure that your detectives, uniformed force, and other special units work together, here are a few tips.

Emphasize the Common Enemy

As units get caught up in their day-to-day responsibilities, they can lose sight of the bigger picture, without regard for the other units. As a commander you can refocus them on the broader perspective and the goals of the entire organization.

Remind them that the common enemy is the criminal element and the common goal of the organization is a safe and orderly community. Reemphasize this perspective often and stress that it takes every unit in the organization, working as a team, to effect the goals of the unit and of the organization.

Recognize Each Group

When joint operations are successful, make an effort to recognize everyone's involvement.

When detectives break a long-time burglar and close 100 + cases, look deeper. It may be that dispatchers "read" into a routine call and quickly dispatched a uniformed unit. The officer caught the burglar fleeing the scene and charged him with one burglary. Excellent interrogation by detectives resulted in the burglar admitting to all the others.

Emphasize that this was a joint effort and acknowledge publicly the excellent performance of each unit toward the common goals of the organization.

Conduct Joint Meetings

Whenever possible, allow the commanders of several units to meet jointly to discuss operations that may affect other units. Allow each to vent any concerns and explain how it will affect their unit or how they may be able to help.

Too often unit commanders don't consider the effect that their individual actions will have on the operations of another unit.

As an example, at a routine joint meeting the head of your surveillance unit announces they are considering the execution of a series of exercises and possible administrative searches in an undercover, administrative sting operation. The undercover detectives will need uniformed support. The uniformed force commander announces that he is already short-handed and stacking calls for service because a national politician is coming to the facility. In addition, the K-9 unit announces it is also short-handed for the same reason, and training has a couple of their people in a school. Better that these problems find solutions before the events than having serious problems occur during the event or lingering animosities between units after the event.

Reduce the Distance Between Units

This can be done both psychologically and physically. Meetings can help the commanders, but the use of joint training and operations can help the rank and file members of the force understand their relationships to other units in the organization.

As a commander, you may also be able to reduce the physical distance between units. In one organization, both detectives and the uniformed officers shared the same floor of the same building. Yet detectives always used the front door, uniformed officers the back door. They seldom crossed paths and virtually never talked. When the commanders of both units realized what was going on, they set the example by freely walking into each other's space and encouraging their subordinates to do the same. Soon both units were sharing information on a daily basis.

In the law enforcement arena, as in life, the higher you go, the more you can see. That increased vision allows you to point out areas to others that they cannot see from their lower vantage point in the organization. Use that vision effectively to build the individual units in your organization into a "lean, mean, crime-fighting machine." The resulting team effort will benefit everyone.

Section 7 — Department Culture — What's Yours Like?

Your police department is unique. It is responsible for policing a one-of-a-kind population for your municipality. Your department differs from others in size, structure, budget, and a host of other descriptors. But perhaps your department's most defining descriptor is that of your departmental culture.

Whenever I am hired to conduct management training by a police department, I always fly in a day early. Once I am settled at my hotel, I get out and take a look at the community to get a feel for what type of policing is being done. More importantly though, I seek out one or more police officers and simply ask for directions back to my hotel. Those brief encounters tell me a great deal about the culture of that department. These encounters help tell me whether there is a progressive, citizen-oriented police force, or an occupying army with an us vs. them mentality.

The following is a list of five components that I consider to be primary in evaluating a police department's culture. The culture of a department, good or bad, is generally a direct function of the quality of its leadership. How does yours stack up?

Attitude

When approached for directions, what are the officers' attitudes? Are they approachable or does their body language deliver a "Don't bother me" message to citizens? Once approached are they friendly or act as if giving directions is not a part of their job description?

How far is an officer willing to go to assist a stranger in the city? "Follow me," is perhaps the most common response that I receive. But I've also heard, "You shouldn't be in this part of the city…," and "What do I look like—an information bureau?"

What would your officers say and do in this situation?

Are you sure?

Appearance

From the officers, to the cars, to the police station, the appearance that the police department projects to the public speaks volumes about your department. Some tipoffs, to me, include dirty and dinged-up cars, and sloppy, overweight, or unkempt officers. When two or more officers are together, are they dressed alike?

The police station or precinct houses also tell me a great deal about what the city fathers think of their police department. Are the building and training facilities new and state-of-the-art or are they old and dilapidated? If the police leadership can't arrange for the proper cleaning of their own buildings, can you really trust them to clean up entire neighborhoods?

Conduct

Police officers generally work with little direct supervision. They travel throughout the community, interacting with all types of people. To be effective, they need to be disciplined in their words and actions.

How they interact with waitresses, clerks, and each other while in the public eye is critical in assessing the culture that governs their conduct—good or bad. Their language, conversation, and general demeanor all reflect directly on the department.

How are your people handling themselves when they are out of your view?

Professionalism

Do your people look, act, and perform like professional police officers? Do they project the image of well-trained, educated, and disciplined protectors of the public? Are they courteous and helpful to all classes of citizens? Are they unbiased and nondiscriminatory in all of their actions and interactions with the public?

Professionalism is a package. Be sure your people are delivering that package to the public—on time, every time.

Public Confidence

The few simple questions I ask local service personnel that I encounter help me gauge the level of public confidence in their police department. It's amazing what people will tell me—a perfect stranger—about the attitudes, encounters, and even the personal lives of their police officers.

Rest assured that your officers are being watched and talked about by the public, both positively and negatively. Even when you discount the very nature of police work as sometimes legitimately coming in conflict with citizens, where there is no public confidence in the police, there can be no effective policing. And a lack of public confidence is a direct reflection of the police leadership of a community.

My brief afternoon or evening encounters with random officers, random cars, and random precinct houses are far from scientific. My brief interviews with a few randomly selected service personnel, of unknown background and status, are also not scientific.

But the impression of the police department that I have at the end of the evening is generally the same impression I get when I meet my class full of your officers the next morning. Those officers' attitudes, appearance, conduct, and professionalism nearly always reflect the department's culture and leadership—good or bad.

How would your departmental culture stack up if I arrived in your community a day early?

Chapter 10
JOB SECURITY

Success usually comes to those who are too busy to be looking for it.
— Henry David Thoreau

Section 1 — Enhancing Your Career Prospects

Section 2 — Moving Up the Ladder

Section 3 — Benefits of Proper Delegation

Section 4 — Managing Stress

Section 5 — Seven Deadly Sins

Section 6 — Are You Being Filtered

Section 7 — Are You a Good Commander?

Section 8 — Self-Evaluation Time

Section 1 — Enhancing Your Career Prospects

You are good at your job, but you feel you need more to get ahead. Your intuition is probably right, but exactly what do you need to do to stand apart from the crowd of other competent members of your department who also want that next promotion?

Here are a few hints based on the successful careers of others in policing.

Keep Learning — Knowledge is Power!

Both technical training and academic education can help enhance your career. Put in a request for any technical school that might enhance your knowledge or understanding of police work. Even if it is not directly related to your present assignment or position, it may give you the background you need for a future promotion or position.

Regarding formal education, the trend is becoming clearer in police work. More and more entry-level positions require a two- or four-year degree. The logic here is that to be in a position for promotion to higher ranks, you need a higher degree than those you will supervise. In many progressive police organizations, sergeants are now expected to have bachelor's degrees, lieutenants are expected to have Master's degrees and higher-level officers are expected to have Master's degrees and additional technical or academic training.

Professional Associations

Upwardly mobile officers participate in police trade associations to receive up-to-date information in the field as well as to network with other professional police officers in other departments.

These organizations often provide magazines and newsletters that discuss current issues, problems, solutions, and trends in policing. Most also have an annual trade show consisting of an opportunity to meet face-to-face with other members to share experiences and knowledge.

Writing

Once you acquire knowledge and experience in policing, it is only natural to want to share your expertise with others in the field. One of the best ways to do that is to write magazine or newsletter articles for trade associations or commercial publications.

Many publications will work with first-time writers who have something of value to share with others in policing. Once you get published, you will find it easier to write and publish other articles.

Writing can get you valuable recognition, as well as opening many doors of opportunity for your career.

Speaking

Communications skills are such a big part of effective management that the ability to speak before groups is almost a requirement for law enforcement supervisors.

A fringe benefit is that the more public speaking you do, the better known you become. Groups will start requesting you personally from your department.

You have to know what you are talking about, prepare thoroughly, and continually polish your delivery, but the experience you gain will be extremely valuable when you face oral boards or assessment centers for promotion. The recognition you will receive as a requested spokesperson from your department will also enhance your position within your agency.

Teaching

Most police academies are constantly seeking qualified and professional officers at all ranks to act as instructors in both basic and in-service schools. If you have prepared yourself well and have the credentials, experience, and a desire to teach, you can dramatically increase your visibility and recognition by teaching.

In addition to police academies, many colleges and universities utilize qualified police practitioners to teach criminal justice classes as adjunct (part-time) professors. This often requires at least a Master's Degree in Criminal Justice or a related field, years of practical experience, and a proven ability to teach. The visibility is high and, as long as you comply with your department's moonlighting regulations, this can be an excellent way to set you apart from your competition in the department.

To be successful and promotable in the field of law enforcement requires a great deal of preparation and development. You can prepare yourself through education, training, and experience. However, to be truly successful, you must reach out to other areas to prove yourself and be recognized as a truly effective and competent leader in the police community.

Section 2 — Moving Up the Ladder

"Moving up the ladder" can have different meanings to different people. Regardless of your rank or your future aspirations, there are basic guidelines for reaching your future goals.

So whether you want to go from sergeant to lieutenant, detective to chief investigator, or chief of a small department to chief of a larger department, heed the following words of advice:

Grow in Your Job

Regardless of the position you now hold, you can effectively grow in your job. First, learn everything you can about *your* job. Become the best that you can be in that position. In doing so, you will become the standard for that position and will be recognized as such by your subordinates, peers, and those of higher rank.

Then, be sure that you know the jobs of others, both below and above you in rank. Learn their duties and responsibilities. Knowing and understanding their jobs, and their relationship to your current job, will help you understand the relationship between various ranks and their relationships to the department.

Broaden Your Experience

Upwardly mobile officers are seldom specialists. To move up the ranks you need broad-based experience within the department.

To gain this experience, you can rotate between various assignments such as uniform, detective, and administrative assignments. You may also want to volunteer for special assignments within your current area to learn the special and unique organizational skills associated with such assignments. The experience and insight gained in such assignments can be of great value as you embark on future special assignments of your own.

Further Your Education

We've said this before, but … it's important! The trend is clear regarding formal education in law enforcement. More and more police and sheriff's departments are requiring college degrees or some level of college credits for entry-level personnel. Some major police organizations actually require a two- or four-year degree for candidates to be considered for the position of police officer.

Given that trend, it is only logical that those who supervise those college-educated police officers should be college-educated themselves.

Therefore, when you go up for promotion, you may be facing candidates who have two- or four-year degrees in criminal justice or a related field. At the rank of lieutenant in many large progressive departments, the majority of candidates will have Master's degrees in criminal justice, public administration, or management.

Despite your extensive practical experience, you may not make the final cut in the competition for that higher rank or new job unless you have the appropriate college degrees.

Get Specialized Training

Being upwardly mobile can mean a variety of things, but certain specialized training can set you apart from the crowd. Whether you want to be a captain or a chief, you must have training in budget preparation. After all, when you are competing for municipal funds, you are pitting your budget justifications against those of other municipal agencies. May the best-prepared budget win!

Other specialized training that can be of great value in setting you apart includes specialty training in human resources management, tactical team management, hostage negotiations, media relations training, and, of course, all aspects of police administration and management.

Prepare for Promotion

From years of observation, it is clear that those who prepare for promotion are the most likely to succeed at getting promoted.

Years ago there were very few programs or products for helping you get promoted. Today, there are books, videos, and courses to help you get through promotional exams, oral boards, and assessment centers. Those officers who take advantage of such resources are much more likely to get promoted in professional departments than those who rely on their own perceptions of what it takes to be promoted.

Promote Yourself

Let it be known that you are interested in moving up the ladder. Confide in your supervisor that you are interested in your own potential for upward mobility. If you are already in a command position, let it be known that you are interested in becoming more upwardly mobile.

Mentors and supporters are only interested in police personnel who want to move forward. They will not waste their time, nor their political capital, in supporting someone who is "iffy" about their professional aspirations.

To that end, promote yourself professionally. Speak to local and civic groups as a professional law enforcement officer. Become known to your local constituents, as well as your local politicians. Support your current police administrators as a loyal member of their team. In short, be a professional and it will reward you in your own professional career.

Network, Network, Network

Law enforcement is, and will continue to be, a person-to-person business. That same person-to-person premise will also help you get promoted within your agency and beyond it.

In order to network, you must be a part of your local constituency, as well as a member of a larger law enforcement community. Your reputation and standing in the law enforcement community are critical to your success in getting promoted. The way you are perceived by your peers and subordinates bears directly on how you are perceived by your superiors and others in a position to promote you.

Join professional police associations, both local, regional, and national. Become an organizational leader, writer, and speaker. Such actions will set you apart from your peers and enhance your image as a police leader.

Network with those you encounter, whether on the local or national level, to share information, experiences, and, of course, promotional opportunities.

Keep in mind that law enforcement is a "human services" business. Emphasizing the "human" part of that business is the key to success in being an upwardly-mobile officer at any rank.

Preparing yourself adequately and cementing the community, departmental, and political relationships that surround you will define your level of success in your career.

Section 3 — Benefits of Proper Delegation

In a previous chapter, we advised you on how to delegate. Here we provide you with the benefits of proper delegation.

Wherever you are on the management ladder of your agency, you must delegate certain tasks to others. Otherwise, you will be overwhelmed by trying to do everything yourself. Yet some law enforcement managers don't delegate enough, and some even try to micromanage their commands.

Understanding the benefits of effectively delegating is key to motivating you to be sure that you do delegate. To help you understand why you should, here is a list of advantages to you and your department.

Ability to Do *Your* Job

A law enforcement manager needs to manage. Proper delegation can give you the time to do your job, to think, to plan, to look to, and provide for the future of your command.

Increasing Your Productivity

A manager's productivity is not measured by what he or she can do. Their productivity is measured in what he or she can manage to get done.

If you are bogged down in routine actions and "administrivia" that other people in your unit could easily handle, you are not as productive as you could be. That is not good for you, your career, or the department.

Appropriate Decision-Making

Decisions in any organization should be made at the lowest possible level. In general, the lowest possible level means the level at which the decision maker has the best facts at the time, place, and circumstances when the decision needs to be made.

Trusting your lieutenants, sergeants, and officers is a critical part of the delegation process. But if you as a commander have properly trained, supervised, and mentored your people, they will make the right decision most of the time without your intervention.

Building an Effective Manager — *You*

As a police manager, you will be judged by your superiors on the effectiveness of your unit overall. Yes, you can personally help your unit by doing its work, but not in the long term.

You can best help your unit succeed by motivating, coaching, maintaining discipline and standards, and the whole host of management responsibilities that require your time and energy. Delegating routine tasks frees you up to do the things necessary to allow you to truly develop your unit and the future leaders within it.

Going Up?

When you properly delegate, you will be recognized as an effective police manager who has leadership abilities. As a leader, you will have properly prepared others in your unit to eventually replace you. That ensures you are promotable to a higher rank, without adversely affecting your current unit.

The last thing you want to see stamped on your promotion request is: "Denied, no suitable replacement."

Improved Communication

Employees want meaningful work and a good relationship with their bosses. The proper delegation of meaningful work makes employees feel worthwhile. At the same time they are gaining valuable experience for a future promotion of their own.

One of the byproducts of the process is that they actually get to interact on a daily basis with you, and they can participate directly in the common goal of accomplishing the overall mission of the unit.

That's good for everyone.

Employee Development

Every law enforcement commander is responsible for developing the skills and abilities of those in his/her unit. Proper delegation helps to develop subordinates' skills, abilities, initiatives, creativity, and competence. There is no substitute for this developmental process in professional police agencies.

Learning to properly delegate tasks and responsibilities requires "letting go" to some degree. But it is also an opportunity to truly work "with" your people. You get to watch them slowly grow, develop, and mature. And someday, they will be ready and capable of taking over your job.

That's okay. Because by that time, you will be promoted and, hopefully, will have them in your command chain; professional and competent commanders, trained by the best—you!

Section 4 — Managing Stress

Is being a law enforcement commander stressful? Yes. Is that stress harmful to you? Not necessarily!

It's all in how you handle it.

The dual demands of police work and management, by their very nature, lead to mental and physical tension. Yet some law enforcement commanders seem to thrive on such stress, while others suffer from burnout or other mental or physical problems. Understanding why some commanders suffer while others thrive could be the key to your long-term survival in your present and future positions.

To help you in your survival, here are a few things that successful commanders do to minimize their stress and its consequences. Follow their actions to be sure you keep your stress level to a minimum.

Be Technically Proficient

Marginally trained police commanders suffer from a variety of stresses. Because of their lack of knowledge about their jobs, they aren't sure what to do, worry about decisions they do make, and often incur the wrath of their superiors for making wrong decisions.

Well-trained and competent police commanders know what to do, when to do it, and they get it done. Then they move on to other challenges, confident that they have done the right thing. Their superiors and subordinates alike tend to trust and respect them and that alone is a stress reducer.

Maintain a Positive Attitude

Optimists see the positive aspects of the world, while pessimists tend to look at the negative aspects of the world. And optimists make the best police commanders. Because they are always "up," their positive attitudes are contagious and spread to subordinates, coworkers, and even their superiors.

Having a positive attitude in general makes it much easier to handle unexpected problems. When they occur, good commanders just view them as a minor obstacle on the road to success. They handle them quickly, positively, and move on.

Don't Expect Too Much

One of the reasons you are a commander is that you were very competent in your previous position. You quite likely performed better than your peers in both quality and quantity of work.

Now that you set the performance standards for your subordinates, recognize that they are not you. They may have neither the drive nor the ability to meet the standards that got you promoted. Yet, they put in a reasonable effort and attain reasonable results for their positions. Setting your expectations at too high a level will increase everyone's stress levels, especially yours.

Take Care of Yourself

The studies and literature are clear regarding what you need to do to effectively handle the inevitable stress of your work. To be successful you must incorporate certain stress-reducing activities into your demanding and hectic life. If you don't, stress will take its toll in the long run.

Eating healthy, well-balanced meals is a necessity. So is ensuring that you get adequate rest, including periodic vacations away from your work and regular routine. Exercise is a must, not only because it tends to reduce general tension, but because being physically fit can add to your sense of well-being, safety, and confidence.

And of course, balancing your life to include work, family, friends, and your personal time is critical to a happy, healthy, and minimally stressful lifestyle.

Maintain Your Sense of Humor

Police work, particularly at the command levels, is serious business. However, it isn't deadly serious all of the time. There is plenty of room in the day for a less intense environment to exist in the workplace.

Although humor must be used carefully in today's workplace, it can be used to keep the situation in perspective as well as allowing everyone to have a little fun at work.

Many commanders find that a bit of appropriate humor at the right time can dramatically reduce the stress and tension of a difficult situation for both themselves and the others involved in the situation.

Don't Be a Source of Stress

Many police commanders fail to recognize that their actions or demands can be serious sources of stress for their subordinates. Just as humor and positive attitudes can be infectious in the workplace, so can stressors.

As the person in charge of your department or unit, you can set the stress tone for others. You can do that by setting realistic goals, reasonable deadlines, and by separating out the serious crises from the routine problems. Following the guidelines set out here can also have the effect of minimizing the stress on your subordinates by minimizing the stress on you.

Yes, being a law enforcement commander has its stresses, but then, that's why you get the big bucks. Properly handling the stress is how you show the world that you deserve those big bucks, and their respect.

Section 5 — Seven Deadly Sins

Although we try to concentrate on the positive aspects of being a law enforcement commander, a survey of over 600 sergeants has unveiled the traits that create the greatest disdain for their commanders.

It is incumbent upon you to ensure that you are not guilty of the following seven deadly sins of police management. Here is what those 600 sergeants said are the worst traits in a police commander.

1. ***Closed-mindedness*** – Whether it's a viewpoint in a criminal case, a complaint against personnel, a new procedure or an innovative product in policing, be sure you approach it with an open mind. Change is inevitable, and a commander's job is to review each recommendation or innovation with an open mind. Your duty is to then evaluate each option based on your education, training, and experience and to project into the future the value of the new ideas, procedures, and processes that you encounter. Keeping an open mind will allow creativity to flourish from below, ensuring that your agency changes with the times.

2. ***Being Two-Faced*** – This criticism is general and can be avoided by simply being honest. Your personal integrity is the most important asset you have in being a successful commander. Protect that asset. Be fair and just with all you encounter, from politicians to subordinates, and you will avoid this two-faced criticism.

3. ***Being Arrogant and Egotistical*** – This allegation forces you to walk a fine line. To be a successful commander, you should appear to be in command. To do this, you must be decisive and self-assured. To some, you may appear to be arrogant and egotistical.

   Work to ensure that you make time to talk with your staff. Find out who they are, what they want and where they are going. If you are an educated, adequately trained, and experienced professional who interjects a reasonable degree of empathy and compassion into your work, you will avoid this type of allegation.

4. ***Abusing Power*** – This allegation is often made by those who may not understand the duties of a person in your position of power. The concept of power relies on the ability to control the actions of others. It is akin to leadership that is getting others to do what you want them to do because they want to do it.

To avoid allegations of abuse of power, fundamental fairness is the rule of power. From the days of King Solomon to your present-day duty decisions, the rule is simple: Be fair to all, follow a fair and just path of action, and as Shakespeare put it, "Thou canst then be false to any man." 

5. ***Inconsistency*** – Poor commanders play favorites, enforce rules selectively, or grant favors to selected individuals. This type of inconsistency undermines a commander's authority. To combat this type of allegation, commanders should treat all members of the command equally, enforce discipline and standards equally, without favoritism or discrimination. Promotions and assignments should be made on the basis of who is best for the job and what is best for the department.

6. ***Holding Grudges*** – For commanders to hold grudges opens them up to a wide variety of future problems and allegations. Problems and confrontations are facts of police work and police supervision. To move beyond them is a mark of professionalism and integrity. Commanders who fail to move beyond the solutions to problems, and who continue to hold grudges, will be held in contempt by their subordinates. The decision is yours. Handle the situation and move on, or be held in contempt for your failure to move on. The decision is yours.

7. ***Not Caring About Your People*** – This allegation is often centered more in perception than in reality. It is true that you must balance your concern for getting the job done against the concern for your people. In the demanding world of policing with limited resources, you must sometimes run short-handed or without other protective resources. However, successful commanders take care of their people whenever possible. To run short-handed should be an unusual situation. To place people in danger should only be done during critical and necessary operations. Keeping your people informed and minimizing their risks can help avoid such an allegation.

Think carefully about which of these traits you might possess from time to time. Think even more carefully about how you might better handle these situations and avoid these seven deadly sins of law enforcement management.

Are you a model of integrity, honesty, and fundamental fairness? Or do you play favorites, hold grudges, and abuse your power as a police commander?

Take time to evaluate yourself as a commander. Your subordinates know the truth—do you?

Section 6 — Are You Being Filtered?

You won't find the management meaning of this term in most dictionaries unless you are very astute. The term filtering generically means to separate out certain things before they reach their destinations. A simple example is when certain light colors are excluded from a picture by use of a filter. The picture arrives at its destination, but with certain elements, in this case colors, missing.

In management terms, filtering means that certain things are removed before the message ever gets to you at your command level. The course of the omission can vary. It may be that commanders below you don't want to deliver bad news to you. It may be as simple as your commanders not wanting to embroil you in their controversy. Or it could be that they are intentionally withholding information from you for some other reason.

Regardless of the motives, every commander needs to protect themselves from the inadvertent or intentional filtering of information to them. To help you avoid any problems associated with filtering, here are a few tips to help ensure you don't become the victim of such filtering.

Pay Attention

As a police commander it is easy to get caught up in the heavy-duty crisis situations that present themselves to you frequently. But between crises, be sure that you know what is happening in the more routine matters of your command.

Good advice is to check every aspect of your operations, at least occasionally. That means from the locker rooms, to the evidence room, to the board room.

Ask Questions

You can be briefed on the facts of a situation without getting the full story from your subordinates. Sometimes their omissions are accidental or they didn't think you needed to know all the details.

Be sure to ask pointed questions about an incident or situation. Insist that your questions receive good, solid answers. Don't give up until you are satisfied that the who, what, where, when, and why of the situation have been presented and answered. Your last question should be, "Is there anything else I need to know about this situation?"

Keep in Touch

This would be the opposite of "out of touch," which is a common phrase used by subordinates to describe some management-level people. To be sure they don't accuse you of that, be involved at all levels of your command.

Learn how that new radio system works so you can actually use it in an emergency. Learn how to operate the new computers, what their capabilities are, and how they actually increase productivity. Keep up to date with new laws, new procedures, and know what your subordinates are learning in their basic and in-service classes.

In other words, "keep in touch."

Don't Kill the Messenger

In a time of crisis, you need all the facts to help you make decisions and control the aftermath. You need subordinates who are willing to bring you all of the bad news without fear of being "jumped on" as the nearest vent for your wrath.

Let your people know that you need all of the facts and circumstances in a bad situation. Accept those facts and circumstances, without passing immediate judgment or placing blame. Accept all of the information in a calm and professional manner. The goal is to solve the problem.

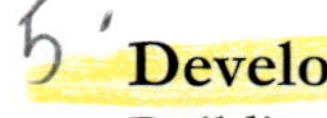

Develop Loyalty

Building the trust and loyalty of your subordinates is a never-ending process that starts the day you show up for work in your new command. Loyalty is a two-way street and your everyday actions are the street signs. Work hard to build up that trust and loyalty—during the easy times—and it will pay multiple dividends during crisis situations.

Filtering is a process that you can avoid with a little work and a lot of common sense. You will know that you are being successful when after being thoroughly briefed about a serious situation, your subordinate ends the briefing abruptly. There will be a slight pause. And then he/she may say, "Sir, there is something else you need to know about this situation."

Section 7 — Are You a Good Commander?

Determining whether or not you are a good law enforcement commander can be difficult. There may be people around you who will praise your virtues no matter what you do. There will also be those whom you will not be able to satisfy no matter how good you really are as a commander.

How are you to cut through these diversions to learn how effective you actually are as a law enforcement commander? The answer is to know what the majority of your personnel want in a commander. Then assume the attributes and accomplishments that are expected of a police commander, leaving the rhetoric behind.

To help you better understand your role, we surveyed 600 police sergeants to find out what they most respected in a good leader. Here are the results of that survey.

Leaders Are Honest

Far and away this is the single most important attribute that police commanders must possess. Subordinates have clearly stated, in several surveys, that their commanders must be honest and have great integrity to be truly effective.

This is easy to achieve. Keep your promises or don't make them. Deal with every person you come in contact with in an honest and straightforward manner. Your reputation will both follow and precede you.

Leaders Have Good Common Sense

Practical problems in policing require practical and workable solutions that require common sense on the part of police command personnel.

But what constitutes common sense? Common sense is the combination of your education, training, and experience that lead to a successful conclusion to the problem at hand. In short, it is whatever works.

Obtaining such common sense is seldom accidental. It is obtained by hard work, studying, attending schools, education, and learning from your and others' mistakes and successes.

Leaders Take Command

A commander who doesn't command is not a commander. Repeated studies have shown that the person who "assumes command" of the situation is viewed as the person in charge. That is either you or someone else. A command vacuum will be filled by you, or a subordinate, or an informal leader.

Leaders Are Fair

A true commander is fair to all: to his superiors, his peers, and the people under his command. He is fair to all, regardless of their race, color, ethnicity, sex, age, or disability. It's not the laws that ensure this—it's the attitude of the commander that ensures this.

Leaders Are Willing to Help

True leaders are always willing to help their personnel and their constituents.

Whether it's clearing red tape for their subordinates or solving problems for their constituents, they are always willing to help in any way they can.

Leaders Are Consistent

Law enforcement commanders can be depended on to do the right thing at the right time. Their subordinates know what to expect most of the time. They know that they need to be neat, clean, starched, and pressed. They know that their commanders, at any rank, will require that they do the right thing at all times, consistent with existing laws, policies, and procedures.

Further, they know that if they do the right thing that their command officer will back their decisions and actions.

Leaders Are Decisive

Nothing is so contemptible as a person who has a command position who is unwilling or unable to make command decisions. Subordinates are much more willing to accept a reasonably correct decision than no decision.

"When in command, take command," is an age-old phrase that is as applicable today as it was in ancient times.

When you took a commander's position, regardless of the rank, you assumed a position of leadership. Therefore, your subordinates expect you to lead.

They will follow your commands, tackle your objectives, and rely on your judgment as long as you show them that you can lead. You can make minor errors, but you must be a credible leader to succeed in the long term.

If you fail to assume your leadership position, or fail to maintain the confidence of your personnel, you will fail in both your objectives and as a leader.

If you assume your leadership role, make reasonable, common sense decisions, and take care of your personnel, you will be a successful commander. As such, you can look for a bright and successful future as an ever-increasingly responsible leader.

Section 8 — Self-Evaluation Time

Knowing oneself is critical to being a successful police commander. To be successful, you must be able to take an objective and realistic look at your own performance. Evaluating your own performance as a police commander will help you to maximize your strengths and minimize your weaknesses in your current position.

In a major survey of police officers, we asked what their commanders did that they viewed as excellent performance.

Here are a few of their responses. Are you living up to their expectations of what they expect from you as a police commander?

Complete this self-evaluation exercise *(...be honest!)*. Rate your own perception of your performance. "1" is bad and "10" is great!

#1 You Set a Good Example

Are you a model police officer, both on and off duty? Are your shoes shined; your uniform clean and pressed; and your car spotless? Are you a professional in all aspects of your personal and private lives? Are you a part of the community that you serve; living there, and contributing to public service activities, both on and off duty?

Your Rating ________

#2 You Manage Correctly

The best managers don't over-manage, nor do they under-manage. The best police managers strike a balance. They give their people the freedom to perform their jobs, and balance that freedom with the proper amount of guidance and control. Do you insist on excellence from your people, and yourself?

Your Rating ________

#3 You Respect Your Subordinates

This trait encompasses both personal and professional respect for your people. How do you respect them, both as people and as officers? Are you unbiased in your everyday actions with *all* of your people and the public?

Your Rating ________

#4 You Are Consistent

As a police supervisor, you enforce rules and regulations equally with all of your people. You don't play favorites and you treat everyone in your unit equally, consistent with their performance.

Your Rating ________

#5 You Have Adequate Experience

To be a successful police commander, you need to have the three building blocks for success: education, training, and experience. Do you have all three in adequate amounts?

Your Rating ________

#6 You Make Decisions

Proper and timely decision-making, based on adequate facts, and circumstances and policies, is a critical area of performance as a police commander.

Your Rating ________

#7 You Are a Good Communicator

Successful police commanders have the ability to communicate with their subordinates, peers, and superior officers, both orally and in written communications, professionally, and with a degree of diplomacy in all directions. Are your total communications skills exceptional or merely adequate?

Your Rating ________

#8 You Teach Your People

Part of your duties as a police supervisor is to ensure that your people know what is expected of them and to ensure that they have the appropriate skills and knowledge to perform their duties. They need you to guide them and make sure that they know the laws, case law, departmental policies, and procedures so that they can feel secure about doing their jobs. Their training is your responsibility. Are you actively living up to that responsibility?

Your Rating ________

#9 You Back Your Subordinates' Decisions

Most of the time you will not be "on scene" to help your people make critical decisions. Are you willing to support your people when they make decisions in the field at the time and place that they make them? Or, are you a "Monday morning quarterback," criticizing the decisions they made in seconds, on the scene, when you weren't there?

Your Rating ________

#10 You Are Honest?

You must be honest to be a successful police supervisor or commander. If you are not honest, you may survive, but you will not have the respect of the good people in your unit. Repeatedly, surveys show that honesty is the number one quality officers want in their police supervisors. Are you totally honest with your people as well as yourself?

Your Rating ________

Add up your score for these 10 traits. __________

Then evaluate yourself according to traditional standards. If you fall below 70%, you should take a serious look at your performance. But, don't be alarmed if you didn't make 100%. Few police supervisors can realistically rate themselves as anywhere near perfect.

Your career is a constant learning experience. Your only failure is in not trying to be better than you are now.

Perhaps the best guidance you ever received on how to have a successful police career came from your mother, your father, or a teacher when they recited a common rhyme:

> "Good, better, best;
> Never let it rest:
> Until the good is better;
> And the better, best."

Best wishes for a long and successful career, and be sure to make your "better," BEST!

Chapter 11
YOUR FUTURE

My will shall shape the future. Whether I fail or succeed shall be no man's doing but my own. I am the force; I can clear any obstacle before me or I can be lost in the maze. My choice; my responsibility; win or lose, only I hold the key to my destiny.

— Elaine Maxwell

Section 1 — Lifelong Learning

Section 2 — Working to Retire

Section 1 — Lifelong Learning

In an information-driven society such as the United States, modern police managers must have a broad-based and deep knowledge of the environment that they operate in on a daily basis. Today's police manager needs a solid background in such diverse areas as personnel law, interpersonal communications, computers, cultural diversity, civil rights laws, and internal affairs procedures, just to name a few.

If you are to flourish in this demanding atmosphere, you must develop a pattern of lifelong learning that will allow you to perform your duties correctly. Many police managers who refuse to "keep up," get out of touch and make serious and sometimes career-ending mistakes; all due to a lack of knowledge of their trade.

Police managers who develop a pattern of lifelong learning about their trade and related subjects will not only gain promotions, they will also gain the respect of their peers, subordinates, and their supervisors. As a result of their knowledge, professional supervisors find it easier to do their jobs, and their people and their supervisors find it easier to trust them as a commander. Lifelong learning really is a win-win-win situation.

Here are a few tips on how to develop a pattern of lifelong learning, for your police career, and beyond:

Trade Magazines and Newsletters

If you are reading this section, you have the general idea. Read whatever you can, not just about your own job, but about police work and police management around the country, and around the world. There are dozens of mainstream police magazines and newsletters. One estimate is that there are nearly 600 police-related magazines, newspapers, newsletters, and blogs in the United States alone. Read a few every month. You will learn a great deal from the experts who write many of the articles.

Seminars

A seminar is essentially a short course on a specific topic. Your annual in-service course, regardless of length, can probably be considered a seminar. Regional academies often provide a menu of courses you can select to fulfill your in-service requirements. But upwardly mobile and professional officers and managers request far more than the minimum requirements. They want more seminars, by better instructors, and they often get approved to attend them. "Ask and ye shall receive," is the operative phrase for success in this arena.

College Education

Would you trust your life to an attorney who had not graduated from law school? Of course not. Would you trust your finances to an accountant who didn't have an accounting degree? You get the picture.

If you want to be a respected professional, get an education in criminal justice, public administration, or some other related field. Yes, I know (because I was there), college is tough because of shift work and other demands of policing. Read on.

Distance and On-Line Learning

Distance learning is freedom. You can learn from the experts, on your hours, and at your pace. You can get reputable and quality training courses, either as a hard copy correspondence or as an online course. Dozens of colleges now offer online Associate's, Bachelor's, Master's, and even Ph.D. degrees online. You never have to go to the college unless you want to march across the stage at graduation. Dozens of seminars and courses on specialty law enforcement topics are offered commercially in the same distance-learning arenas.

Command Colleges

A command college is a specialty school for upwardly mobile police managers. The Southern Police Institute and the FBI's National Academy offer weeks of in-house training courses geared specifically for the development of police commanders. There are several other command colleges offered by other institutions or through state-sponsored schools. Seek them out if you are serious about going up the ranks of your department. In most cases, the department will send you and pay all your expenses. "Serious candidates only" need apply.

Other Learning Opportunities

Police work is a tiny segment of our society and, to be successful, you need a broader base of knowledge than merely police work. Seminars on finance and investments can help you reach retirement early, or at least give you the option. Seminars that help you win friends, influence people, or help you gain another point of view will all make you a better person and ultimately a better, more knowledgeable, and more understanding police commander. And all those skills can be transferred to the private sector when your police career ends, whether suddenly due to disability, disease, or through the retirement system.

The choice is yours. Choosing a pattern of lifelong learning through reading, classes, and college can put you far ahead of other officers for promotions, respect, and a bright future. Choosing to learn what you are forced to learn, attending only required courses, and keeping a narrow focus will get you unemployed, sooner or later.

Best wishes for a long and successful career.

Section 2 — Working to Retire

Police officers of all ranks find themselves in a position to retire from police work at relatively young ages. In most cases that retirement is voluntary. In some cases that retirement may be involuntary. Injuries, health problems, and politics can all be responsible for early retirements.

The question is: Are you prepared for retirement? The goal of being prepared for your inevitable retirement is not necessarily in opposition to your success in your current police position. In fact the goals of the two positions can easily be mutually beneficial. If you haven't thought about it in-depth, then consider the following issues:

Being the Best

Perhaps the best preparation for a second career is to be the best you can be in your first career of police work. Future employers will be impressed by retirees who have already been successful in one career. That success will be measured by the rank you have attained, the training you have had, and the level of education you obtained while with the police department.

If you were the best administrator, investigator, or commander, those successes will be reflected in your records and references. Mediocrity in any position is not noteworthy. It is not the material of an outstanding reputation, nor the subject of enthusiastic references. With serious competition for each worthwhile position in the private sector, you will want all the aces you can muster when approaching your second career.

Retire "To," Not "From"

Looking forward to retirement is not necessarily the same as looking forward. Those who view their relatively early retirement as an escape from the rigors of police work often find themselves "outside" with very limited employment options. That's because they haven't properly prepared for their second career.

The most forward-looking members of the police community recognize that they will be entering into a second career. In most cases, that is a job working under a different set of rules than the paramilitary environment of police work. Although the second career may be less stressful and less demanding, it is something to retire "to," not just an escape from the demands of police work.

Developing Skills

While with the police department, you should make every effort to develop a wide variety of technical, supervisory, and command skills. Although some specialty areas may be marketable in the private sector, there may be a limited call for SWAT team commanders, bomb disposal specialists, crime prevention coordinators, and other police-specific positions.

However, generalists with a wide variety of skills may be more attractive to the private sector. In addition to developing your technical skills, be sure to work on your "people skills." Your ability to supervise and lead people, and your ability to work in a team environment are important attributes to have when seeking employment in the private sector. Be sure that your honesty and integrity are above reproach and that you maintain a reputation as a professional in all aspects of your police career. That's good both on and off the job.

Your Personal Attributes

Although you may spend 20 to 30 years in police work, recognize that many of the attributes that have made you successful in police work are readily transferrable to other jobs. These include your ability to get the job done, your discipline, and your enthusiasm. The private sector needs people with these attributes. Companies are always looking for honest, dedicated, disciplined, professional employees at all levels. Take inventory of your skills and attributes and you will feel very confident about your ability to succeed in another career.

Credentials

Regardless of how good you are, you may not even make the first cut for a new position unless you have credentials that are equal to or better than your competition for the same position. Your credentials can include college degrees, certificates of specialized training, courses you have taught, special licenses you hold, and, of course, your personal references, both formal and informal.

Throughout your police career, you should keep a "running resume" that includes all of these credentials. Your running resume may be of great value on some occasions while you are in police work, but it will be an absolute necessity when you leave police work.

Networking, Networking, Networking

As you progress through your police career, you should make an effort to interact with, get to know, and keep in contact with police officers and civilians from many departments and agencies. Too many police officers and commanders get caught up in their everyday departmental activities, to the exclusion of the outside world.

Make a special effort to make and keep contacts, inside and outside your department, who are themselves sharp, and therefore upwardly mobile. The captain from another department you worked with on an internal affairs investigation may be the next chief of a major department and looking for a sharp deputy chief. And the detective you worked with on a joint homicide investigation may become the chief investigator for a major insurance company.

Preparing for retirement doesn't mean disloyalty to your current department. In fact, while preparing for your inevitable retirement, you will be building skills, education, and training that are applicable to, and an advantage for, your current department. Whether you move on to another police department, a private security position, or take the plunge into the corporate world, you need to prepare by being the best you can be in your current position.

Whether in your current police position or in your dream retirement job, adequate planning and preparation will make it all much easier and more enjoyable.

Chapter 12
EPILOGUE

Congratulations! You have finally reached the end of this book. We sincerely hope you have gained some insight and knowledge about being a professional law enforcement manager.

But your quest does not end here.

Tomorrow you will be confronted by new personalities, new technologies, and an ever-changing set of laws, personnel practices, and social anomalies.

To maintain your professionalism as a law enforcement manager, you will be forced to adapt to that ever-changing work environment. If you can do that successfully, you will continue to succeed and thrive throughout your career.

However, if you fail to adapt, you may find yourself getting pushed into the "tar pit" with the rest of the dinosaurs!

As a parting comment, we sincerely hope we have been able to give you some guidance and direction toward achieving a successful career in law enforcement, whether through this book or the others that we have written.

Best wishes for a long and successful career!

Mike and Roger

You've achieved success in your field when you don't know whether what you are doing is work or play.
– Warren Beatty

Index